D0056457

THE LONG SHADOW OF SMALL GHOSTS

MURDER *and* MEMORY
in an AMERICAN CITY

LAURA TILLMAN

SCRIBNER

New York   London   Toronto   Sydney   New Delhi

Scribner
An Imprint of Simon & Schuster, Inc.
1230 Avenue of the Americas
New York, NY 10020

First Scribner hardcover edition April 2016

SCRIBNER and design are registered trademarks of The Gale Group, Inc.,
used under license by Simon & Schuster, Inc., the publisher of this work.

For information about special discounts for bulk purchases, please contact Simon &
Schuster Special Sales at 1-866-506-1949 or business@simonandschuster.com.

The Simon & Schuster Speakers Bureau can bring authors to your live event.·
For more information or to book an event, contact the Simon & Schuster
Speakers Bureau at 1-866-248-3049 or visit our website at www.simonspeakers.com.

Interior design by Jill Putorti

Manufactured in the United States of America

10   9   8   7   6   5   4   3   2   1

Library of Congress Cataloging in Publication Data is available.

ISBN 978-1-5011-0425-1
ISBN 978-1-5011-0430-5 (ebook)

To my family

Contents

THE
LONG SHADOW
OF SMALL GHOSTS

The Building at 805 East Tyler Street
(Photo by Brad Doherty)

CHAPTER 1

An Unmeasured Feeling

It's a long story here.
—MINERVA PEREZ, NEIGHBOR

Midway through my first year as a newspaper reporter, I walked through a two-story apartment building in Brownsville, Texas, where a poor young couple had murdered their three children. My assignment was to write about the local debate as to whether the decrepit but historic building should be demolished. It sat on a corner on the outskirts of Brownsville's downtown, just a handful of city blocks from Mexico. There, tropical birds effortlessly crossed into the United States from points south, while human travelers traversed international bridges or paid *coyotes* to hustle them surreptitiously across the Rio Grande. Yet, even among the quotidian dramas of the border, the deaths of Julissa, John Stephan, and Mary Jane were not merely reported—they were communally grieved.

When I interviewed people about the murders, some cautioned that the crime was a black hole that held nothing within. Heinous crimes are like that, people said. They do not teach lessons, they only confirm the worst suspicions about what can happen in our world. To venture close to an entity so dark and try to wrest value from its depths was not only foolish, it was dangerous: a black hole withholds and mangles all it consumes and devours anything wandering too close to its invisible mouth. Yet, the same people who compassionately issued this warning also told me, often at length, of all the crime had come to mean in their lives, how it had challenged their beliefs or fortified them. How it continued to flicker as a figure on the edge of their peripheral vision, moving out of range when they turned to see it head-on.

That the victims were children, that the father was from Brownsville, that an explanation seemed always out of reach, had caused people to question their understanding of their community, their spirituality, the values they held as universal. As they reckoned with these questions, they necessarily reconfigured the world around the shape of the crime in its wake.

As I began to visit the building with increasing frequency, I noted a cloud hovering overhead—an accumulation of meaning more dense and persistent than I'd ever intuited. It signaled that there was more to this story than the simple details, the dates and quotes and analysis that a reporter usually assembles. The cloud was heavy with palpable ambivalence, an existential dread about what had happened here and how it had burrowed through and ruptured the landscape, leaving damage that had yet to be completely measured. I began to realize that, if I wanted to comprehend this city, a place layered with unwritten history that seemed to lie naked and obscured in the same instant, this story was key.

I had never before been drawn to tragic crimes. Like many people,

2

I pushed them out of mind when I could. It was easier to box them up and store them on a mental shelf of humanity's worst moments. Media cover these stories for a while, until the case is closed and the criminal is punished. Then, more often than not, the stories retreat into the background, at least on a national level. For the cities that survive them, what changes? Something must change, even if the difference is unnoticeable on the surface. People continue with their lives, having families and teaching their kids. They fall in love and break up. They get degrees and jobs and build new homes. As for the criminals, I figured they still eat and sleep and talk and think.

John Allen Rubio, the father of the children, had become an infamous figure in Brownsville, known by all three of his names. He was both a product of the city, born and raised, and seemingly its communal enemy, guilty of an act almost too terrible to make sense of. He pleaded not guilty by reason of insanity, lost, and was sentenced to die. After winning an appeal, his second trial took place seven years after the crime. Again, he was convicted and was given the death penalty.

When I started writing to John, I didn't expect him to respond. But he wrote to me for years. He told me about his childhood, his depression, and the three children who died that night and early morning. I never fully got used to those envelopes from the Polunsky Unit, sitting alongside the bills and catalogs in our mailbox. John's answers to my questions were candid and conversational in a way I found captivating. He was a confessed killer, but his personality leaped from the pages, undeniably human, full of ideas and memories. In my mind's eye, I could see the curtain at the edge of the proscenium being tugged away. A construct of this man's life had been built by headlines and court documents, but it was complicated, predictably, by his reflections, his language, his version of that life.

After that first tour, I fell into the building's orbit. I'd drive by on my way home from work and pause for a long moment at the stop sign out front. Later, I would park and walk around the perimeter slowly, cataloging its every corner and blemish and frailty. The cloud lingered here, whether the sky was dense with fog or crisp and blue. Someday, John and the building would be banished from the earth. It felt as if everything were disappearing, or about to, until all that would be left was a sad story with no meaning.

There had to be meaning; it hung morosely overhead. I could feel it following me, leaving a damp film on my skin when I got home.

I began to compile evidence about what had happened on East Tyler Street and its aftermath and sort through it. The collection came to include more than just the testimony and confessions from the murder case. Much of what I considered evidence was tangential: a house where John lived as a boy, the moral claims of the district attorney who prosecuted the case, the arguments made by people in the neighborhood for why the building should be destroyed. Confounding questions emerged, ones I'd never before considered, which couldn't be resolved by searching a database or conducting a few interviews. Like the algorithm marked in chalk on a mathematician's blackboard, or the brew in a cauldron, it seemed that if the correct elements were fused, they would deliver the answers.

As I was compiling this collection, a letter from John arrived. It contained a request—for a comic book. His birthday was coming up, he said. He would be thirty-two, nearly ten of those years spent in prison as he went through the appeals process. I imagined him, as I often had over the previous year, sitting in a cell I conjured from Hollywood, wishing for a simple gift, a fleck of life as the days dimmed to black.

The comic was called *Rosario+Vampire, Season II, Issue 9*. It would be easy and inexpensive to send, and John told me he'd continue writing and answering my questions either way. The phrasing of the request, "Would it be wrong for me to ask you a favor?" struck a chord. Yes, I wanted to reply, this is not how the journalist-subject relationship works. But I'd never interviewed a person on death row before. I might be one of his only connections to the world beyond his cell.

I often felt grateful to John during the time we corresponded. I had hundreds of questions, and he did his best to answer them, sometimes breaking responses down into several letters to get to the whole list. I imagined he got something out of the exchange; there wasn't much else to occupy the twenty-two hours he spent alone in his cell each day. Maybe it made him feel important to know someone was interested in the intricacies of his life story, his opinions, feelings, and memories. Still, he remained justifiably cautious as he wrote to me.

I have never spoken to any media member since this thing all happened and I will be frank and say that the reason that I have not is because it would not matter what I say be it true or false it will always be printed in a way that will make me look like more of a monster taht I already look as. I do not trust any media at all but

I will give you a chance to show me if I have been wrong about my view on this because I can not blaim you for what others have done and said about me.

Beyond the implicit terms he was laying out—I won't prejudge you, don't prejudge me—John also made two explicit requests in that first letter. He asked me to convey his words the way he meant them. He also told me to ask no questions about the crime itself, though in later letters he began to volunteer that information as well. Maria Angela Camacho, his common-law wife, who was also convicted for her part in committing the murders, was serving three concurrent life sentences and would be eligible for parole in 2045. She did not respond to my letters.

My correspondence to John was businesslike. I asked him lists of questions and thanked him for writing back. I didn't talk about myself or try to create a meaningful relationship. I didn't want to give John the impression that I was trying to get him released or get his sentence changed. False hope seemed the cruelest currency.

But when he asked for the comic book, I wondered if I wasn't being cruel in a different way. When I spoke to people outside the world of journalism, I watched their expressions change when I mentioned it. They regarded journalism's ethical rules skeptically, like the intolerant and rigid laws of a fundamentalist religious sect. The comic book might not be a symbol of manipulation. Instead, giving this gift to John could be an act of uncomplicated compassion. Maybe it didn't merit so much debate.

A month passed and another letter arrived. This one was filled with newspaper clippings—puzzles and articles with little cartoons in the margins. One article showed a picture of a baby beluga whale being fed from a bottle. Above the headline John wrote, "So sweet dinner time yum yum. Just a baby. Jesus is great."

In the letter, John said the comic book had arrived and he didn't know whom it was from: "I really did not want to ask you for anything it is just that I reeeaally wanted this book and now I do. If it was not you this is acquered!? Well, who ever did send it I am very happy."

It wasn't from me. I'd never made my decision.

Rosario+Vampire, which I then ordered to see what John was reading, is a Japanese comic book series about a boy named Tsukune, who, because of his poor test scores, transfers to a private school and soon learns his new classmates are monsters hiding in human bodies. He becomes the force of good in a dangerous place, despite his trouble in school.

Japanese manga is not my genre of choice, and I had trouble getting through it, with its dozens of characters to keep track of and constant fight sequences. I don't get the adolescent boy's thrill of seeing a curvaceous anime succubus inked on the page. But it quickly became clear why John might feel a kinship with Tsukune. John, too, had struggled through school. He wanted to join the army after graduation, but couldn't pass the exam. Instead he was cast out into the unpredictable world of adulthood in a poor neighborhood in the poorest area of the country. In March 2003, just a few years after he graduated from high school, he killed his children and those of his common-law wife, claiming they were possessed by demons at the time of their death. In his narrative, he's the good guy thrust into a world where evil can inhabit any form, even children. While his actions seem sinister to us, he knew that he had no choice.

As I learned more from John about his life, I also researched the horrific act he committed once he nailed the door to the apartment shut. Over time, I became accustomed to the account of the murders and started to believe I could analyze them impartially. Then I'd learn a new detail—something small and seemingly insignificant—and suddenly the scenario would be brought back into sharp, sickening reality. It became, again, not simply a generic story of horror, but a living, breathing scene, crawling up my back, insinuating itself in my brain. Another letter from John would arrive in the mail. I'd look at it skeptically and hold it at a distance.

I wrote back to John and told him that, no, I was not the one who'd bought him the comic book. But in the following letter, he asked for the next installment in the series. "I would be soooo grateful to you, indebted to you even." The word "indebted" grated. I didn't want to be in John's debt, and I didn't want him to be in mine, answering my questions with the hope of gaining something material. I told him I'd never given a source anything before and didn't want to start now.

It would have been easier to make this decision with any other subject before John. There would have been no conflict. The rules of journalism, though often requiring thought, are fairly clear and defined. But if the point of learning about this story was to allow it to breathe, I could not seal this man in a box on that shelf of unimaginable things.

John and I were caught together in the same constellation. I'd sought it out; I'd crowded close to a story to which I had no innate right. It was his family, his trial, his town. It was his life and his death. But, as I began to learn how the crime continued to affect those around me, I realized that this was not an isolated act, but a wave moving out in all directions, pushing on those in its path. I'd always believed that I was stuck in the same celestial soup as every other living soul. Until then, I'd never had proof.

It seemed especially unkind to deny John a comic book, after he'd told me about the only new thing his father had ever given him—a bicycle: "It had a banana seat that had gold glitter, a little girly but it was a beautiful bike. I hugged and kisse dmy dad alot that day."

Even that memory turned into a chronicle of unhappiness. John wrote that his grandmother had demanded he keep the bike outside during the night, even though he insisted it would be stolen. In the morning, the bike was gone: "Never did get anything new again nor ever saw that bike again."

Two decades later, kids continue to bike the streets where John grew up, and through alleys where papaya trees grow. When the sun rises, many eat *nopalitos*, a paddle-shaped cactus, sliced from a twisting plant and scrambled into eggs. Or, they wait until school for the tamales or biscuits provided by the district.

Downtown, prostitutes wait to be picked up on street corners after dark, the Immaculate Conception Cathedral observing them from above, near warehouses stuffed with mountains of used clothes discarded by residents in New York or Louisiana. When the piles are sorted, the clothes are displayed in the windows of Brownsville shops, or on front lawns across the city at permanent garage sales, or carried across the bridge by the kilo to be resold in Mexico. For many children in Brownsville, the appearance of a new thing in their lives, such as a bicycle flecked with gold glitter, is a moment not soon forgotten.

Much has changed here since John's youth, and with people coming across the border constantly, the population is always in flux. But some things have held, and the tight grip of poverty is chief among them. Kids here still wake up to find that something has been taken from them, be it a bike or a parent who has been detained.

As I sought to understand what this case meant to the city, people began to reveal what they cared deeply about—the precious gems of insight, history, love, and hate usually kept from strangers like me. Murder and bloodshed were not included on the list, though at times these traumas obscured what was most important. But the aftermath—a fluttering vision of what the world would look like next—contained multitudes. There I encountered the questions, many of them unwieldy, that drove me into conversations I'd never before had with myself. I began to realize that this pursuit would not produce ready answers, ones that were clean and could quickly be filed away. But this murkiness, while troubling, made me even more committed to continuing these conversations, as they led into surprising and difficult territory.

In time, I sent John money for the supplies he needed to write to me, but I never mailed him a comic book, or any other gifts. I am not sure if this is what fairness looks like precisely, or if such a thing exists.

I continued sifting through the landscape, excavating bits of the architecture left behind, like an archeologist at some not-so-ancient dig site. I pushed the pieces I found into the sunlight, holding them against everything else, allowing them to exist as part of a single picture. Then I tried to dismantle the frame of that picture, so that the story stopped being an account, a report, a myth, and started to mingle with the texture of reality.

CHAPTER 2

An Education

Is there any such thing as an evil building?
—MARK CLARK, MEMBER OF THE BROWNSVILLE HERITAGE COUNCIL

The first time I stepped into the building on East Tyler Street, I held a tape recorder in my hand and was flanked by two photographers. We were on assignment for *The Brownsville Herald*, and I was working on a story about an unfamiliar building that the city was hoping to destroy.

In 2008, the old brick apartment building sometimes called Hotel Imperial or Hotel de los Chiflados—Hotel of the Stooges—by its neighbors, was less than half-occupied. Together, photographers Brad, Daniel, and I walked the few short blocks from the paper and through the unlocked entrance. They began to snap pictures of every detail—the stairs, the bars on the windows, the empty hallway. Every inch that was accessible was recorded by the soft clicks of camera shutters. We were documenting the building because of John and Angela's crimes, but at the time I felt little emotion about the assignment. When I walked through the hallways, the hairs on my neck did not stand on end. I simply held out the recorder and captured tape of my sandals slapping the stairs as I ascended, preparing the audio for a slide show I was to make for the paper's website.

Brad sensed something different. He was entering a landmark, one he'd documented during its darkest hours, when neighborhood children left stuffed animals at a makeshift shrine out front, and the apartment was sealed up as evidence. But most of his photos had been shot from the exterior, the way the majority of the community experienced the building. Now he was within it, and he walked through the hallways with a care and attentiveness that approached reverence.

We peeked inside empty rooms on the second floor. A few stray items had been left behind. A wire hanger and a religious calendar. A sign for the men's bathroom with an oversize playing card—a jack of hearts—pinned up next to it. I tried to talk to a couple of the remaining tenants. One opened the door, heard out our request for an interview, then closed it with a few muttered words. Another spoke vaguely about her desire to stay. I couldn't tell who was living in the building lawfully and who might be squatting, which apartments were occupied and which had been abandoned years ago, after tenants were spooked by what had taken place.

We walked back down the staircase and into the sun. Brad and Daniel had gotten good photographs—the building was full of the idiosyncrasies that make interesting pictures.

On our way back to the *Herald*, I stopped to interview Minerva Perez and Alejandro Mendoza, the building's neighbors. Both elderly, they had lived in their homes in the little barrio nearly their whole lives. Minerva, a sweet and accommodating woman with an open smile and short hair dyed red, felt strongly about the building.

She didn't like to walk on the same side of the street when she passed by, a constant inconvenience because she lived two doors down. Since that March day when the bodies were discovered and the street was swarmed with police, Minerva had urged the county commissioner for her district to tear the building down.

Alejandro, on the other hand, was unaffected. "They hear noises, they hear babies crying," he said of the other neighbors. "They move out of here."

For Alejandro, a hunched, soft-spoken widower, it was about "them," not him. He didn't hear spooky noises, he didn't care much whether 805 East Tyler remained or came down. It had been present his whole life, and the murders didn't change the way he felt. His home, a small wood house painted blue, abutted the side of the building. Pragmatically, he saw this as an advantage: the wall provided protection from cold fronts during the winter. Alejandro described himself as someone who "never liked anything." Other people liked to dance, go to movies, spend time outside, but not him. He wasn't enthusiastic about life, and that extended to his feelings about the building, where his late wife had worked as a maid in the early days of their courtship.

Later that day, I interviewed Mark Clark, a transplant to Brownsville who had opened an art gallery downtown after leaving a career at the Smithsonian. Clark sat on the Brownsville Heritage Council and was skeptical about the plan to tear the building down. To him, the city was attaching a stigma to a structure—a collection of bricks and concrete.

"I feel that the building is getting a death sentence for the crimes of its occupants," he said. "Is there any such thing as an evil building?"

Clark said he was the only member of the Brownsville Heritage Council to vote against the demolition permit, and he was frustrated with his fellow committee members. If it were up to him, demolition of any of the city's antique buildings would be avoided at all costs, regardless of whether they were especially attractive or could lay claim to a famous lineage. Instead, he said such permits were granted regularly, allowing Brownsville's architecture to be slowly, almost imperceptibly depleted, until only the best-financed restoration projects remained. In such a poor city, it might take decades to get beyond the upper echelon of preservation initiatives and finally begin to work on homes that were less architecturally or historically significant, but still helped Brownsville retain its identity. Any building over fifty years of age is worthy of special consideration if a city wishes to use federal funds for its alteration or demolition, according to the Texas Historical Commission, though structural integrity and significance are also weighed to assess the import of preservation.

Over my years in the Rio Grande Valley, I lived in several homes—historic, suburban, and modern. After I arrived from the Northeast, my first home in Brownsville was on the north side of town in a subdivision. The house was not well cared for, but it was relatively new, located in a safe, middle-income area where families with modest means bought modest homes.

At night I'd drive home, feeling as if I were entering an anonymous part of America. The houses could have been in most any city, styled by a faceless architect. But the subtropics persistently encroached, even in the subdivision. A kigelia tree leaned over the back fence, its banana-size seedpods dangling from its branches like earrings, and a tarantula sometimes stood guard on the front stoop.

Brownsville's downtown, where the Tyler Street building is located, is the opposite of the sterile subdivision. In the morning on my way to work, I'd drive off the highway and see a lake on my right, where anhingas and egrets and pelicans, clean and white against the muddy water, dove for meals. Then, the side of the zoo, with just enough wildness peaking over the top of the fence to suggest a foreign universe inside. I'd see the park to my left and the federal courthouse, and then turning toward work, the peeling paint on the small houses beaten down by weather and lack of care, and the purple petals of a tree I couldn't name, the parrots cawing and flashing green in front of my windshield, the lonely dog with the floppy teats weaving out of the street, done with nursing but not ready for death.

I spent just five days in my next residence. I'd convinced the owner to allow me to rent out the finished rooms of a historic house that was undergoing renovation, an idea that quickly proved untenable. I could manage the nails and the sawdust on the floors, but when a swarm of termites descended on my bedroom, I realized I had to find a new place to live.

Next came the Sethman Building, an eight-unit brick apartment building on the lake with the pelicans and anhingas, a half mile from downtown. It was my favorite part of Brownsville, the palm-lined boulevard bordered by grand old homes, tropical trees, and Spanish-revival ironwork. The apartment complex—two buildings joined by an arch—somehow made it into the mix once upon a time, perhaps for visitors who wanted a vacation bungalow on the lake.

To say the word "lake" is also a misnomer. In the Rio Grande Valley, these oxbow lakes, bands of the Rio Grande that have since disconnected from their mother river, are called resacas. Now, most are stagnant. You wouldn't want to swim in one, or even dip your toe. But they create an endemically scenic landscape for the city, a sense that it's woven together around the remnants of a once-raging river that's petered out to a gently flowing shadow of its former self. These resacas give Brownsville a singularity that reveals itself with casual grace, as you watch a great blue heron crane its neck against the buttery light at sunset. Sitting beside a resaca in the warm evening, the city's beauty becomes undeniable, even in the roughness of its poverty, all its edges frayed.

The Palm Boulevard apartment was charmingly eccentric. Everything was white or beige—the walls, the carpets, the kitchen tile, the claw-foot bathtub, the wicker chairs on the porch. In the backyard, a towering avocado tree dropped green jewels of fruit. Termites gnawed at the window frames, and an army of pharaoh ants set up camp inside the walls. The faux-wood tiles of the kitchen floor would come unglued and shift beneath my feet, and in the summer the kitchen became a sauna whenever I cooked because the air conditioner was at the opposite end of the apartment. The screened-in porches gave me a front row seat to Palm Boulevard, and to the woodpeckers that made a home in the trunk of a dead palm tree.

Before I moved to Brownsville, murders were distant events, painted by the homogenous voices of TV anchors. They didn't have much to do with me, and I didn't see any frailty in maintaining a respectful distance. Working in journalism quickly narrowed that space.

After five months at the *Herald* I covered my first murder, in part assigned to me because I'd taken an interest in local women's issues, and the story was of teen-dating violence at its most extreme.

Brenda Lee Nuñez was an academic star, scheduled to graduate from high school early. She was dating a young man, Hector, who was wildly fixated on her, and from all appearances the two were in love. He would call and text her constantly whenever they were apart. Then he began to criticize her body, and soon she began skipping meals and surviving off diet drinks.

Brenda's family got her away from Hector on a vacation, and in the space of that separation, they were able to communicate with her about the danger he posed. When she returned, Brenda broke it off. Hector found a new girlfriend and Brenda was happy, believing he wouldn't bother her again.

But Hector never stopped thinking of Brenda. After he broke up with his new girlfriend, he started asking Brenda out again. She said no, and one Saturday morning in February he came to her house, went up to her bedroom, and tied her up. He raped her and stabbed her twenty-eight times. She was seventeen.

Shortly after the murder, I stood on the family's doorstep. To my surprise, Brenda's family let me into their kitchen and talked with me while they sat stuffing poblano peppers with white cheese. Her death was raw, and I could barely imagine their living in that house under her bedroom, still splattered with blood. They seemed shell-shocked, preparing for a new reality without their daughter. They remembered what led up to the murder—how the mother of the killer had reasoned with them to please convince their daughter to take back her son. He loved her so much.

The next murder I wrote about was of a man who'd been found

by the side of a country road. Police said it looked as if he'd been dragged by a vehicle. It was a Saturday, and my boyfriend drove with me to the edge of town where the police had blockaded the road. We didn't find much besides the tall grass and a ditch. The suspect hadn't been identified and his profile was generic: Hispanic male in his twenties. Without the details, what was there to glean from such a death? Had he died there, in this ditch? Or did the story of his death happen far away?

The next victim was someone I knew. Barry Horn, the director of the Brownsville Museum of Fine Art, was a cheerful man in his late fifties with a coif of blond hair and the charisma of the TV personality he once was in Houston. One of his friends described him to *The Brownsville Herald* as Houston's Truman Capote.

Barry was found stabbed to death outside his bedroom in his home the day of the museum's annual gala. The circumstances of his death—killed by a young man who police said might have been his lover—confused those who knew him. They couldn't believe that the person they held in such high esteem could be secretly dating a nineteen-year-old. Could the story the killer told—that Barry had raped him and the killing had been done in retribution—hold any seed of truth?

I was out of town, visiting friends, when another reporter called and gave me the news. But the story couldn't be conveyed in that conversation. Barry's dead. They're calling it homicide. Found in his house.

The day his body was discovered, his friends and colleagues went on with the gala Barry had planned. As the guests arrived at the museum, dressed to the nines and ready to eat good food and drink champagne, they asked for Barry, to give a word of congratulations. People always looked for him at events like this. He was uncommonly good at small talk, always ready with a funny anecdote, a kind word, or an introduction to someone with common interests. Instead, the gala attendees were informed of his death. Soon, the police would be searching a resaca for the murder weapon.

I returned to Brownsville from New York in time for his funeral. The crowd was large, perhaps a hundred people. I took my turn walking to the front of the church and saw him laid out, skin waxy and false with his eyes closed, missing the whole thing. He'd been murdered. The fact gripped me, a cold hand around my throat.

Untimely deaths rattle us, cause us to question our priorities. Murder unhinges at a deeper level. Barry's life and death lacked finality, and a mystery lay at its heart: why and how he died. A film reel projected in my mind. The drawn-out pain of more than seventy stab wounds, those lonely, terrifying last moments of life. Finally, the adrenaline dissipating, a veil of darkness falling, until the world was blotted out.

Generally, crime coverage didn't fall to me, and I wasn't especially attracted to it. I wrote about the university, politics, culture, art, and health. I spent weekends at festivals, concerts, exhibitions. I learned many more good stories than bad. I boarded a tiny plane and braced myself while an elementary-school student trained on a flight-simulation program took her first try at piloting a real airplane. I visited the *colonias*, where residents had waited for decades for paved roads and indoor plumbing, but managed to prepare their children for college, and I saw schools train their chess teams to compete at the national level. During my first month on the job, I boarded an eighteen-wheeler filled with donated supplies after flooding devastated the Mexican state of Tabasco and watched the country unfurl for thirty hours through a tiny window before visiting refugee camps and lush countryside. I made true friends, at last, and was welcomed into their families. That's how I discovered that the Rio Grande Valley is a lonely place only if you don't have a family of your own.

But murders occupy a specific space in a newsroom, and when a new killing occurred, my colleagues at the *Herald* would often recount stories they deemed more sinister or bizarre from days gone by. I'd sit at my desk in the small, aging building and ask questions. The faces of the other reporters registered emotions from decades past: the shock and wonder, the sadness, the disgust, and the triumph in bringing criminals to justice. Emma, the senior investigative reporter, perpetually wore a black sombrero and a dark poncho. *"Ay, chinelas!"* she'd say, releasing her raspy smoker's laugh. The expression was her PG version of a common Mexican swear word.

High on the list were the stories of Mark Kilroy and Joey Fischer, both young men full of promise and possibility, killed in 1989 and 1993, in disconnected and startlingly strange circumstances. Joey went to Saint Joseph Academy, the wealthy private school hidden in the historic subdivision near my apartment on Palm Boulevard. Joey was a senior, eleventh in his class, immediately accepted to the University of Texas honors program. He was a popular, good-looking boy who had a facility with language. Getting ready for school one morning, he was gunned down in his driveway. He had briefly dated Cristina Cisneros and, when they broke up, her mother, Dora, visited Maria Mercedes Martinez, a folk healer, who saw clients at a secondhand clothing store. When Maria told Dora that Joey didn't want to marry her daughter anymore, Dora asked Maria to cast a spell on Joey. She refused. Dora came up with a different plan. She asked Maria to help her assassinate Joey. Maria advised another of her clients that his marital problems would be solved once Joey was dead. The client hired two other men to complete the job, with the agreement that Dora would pay $3,000. The story was chronicled by Marie Brenner, Joey's cousin, in a September 1993 edition of *The New Yorker*.

Hearing this story in its barest essence is like taking a slippery trip down the rabbit hole. It sounds more like the stuff of a soap opera than a real-life transgression. Joey's life was ended with a few abrupt gunshots that morning as he stood cleaning the windshield of his mother's car in his sunny suburban neighborhood.

Another young man, Mark Kilroy, came to Brownsville during spring break of 1989 while he was attending the University of Texas at Austin. College kids commonly walked to Matamoros for a night of partying and easy underage drinking at the clubs and bars near the international bridge. Usually damage to students was limited to hangovers, maybe a risky liaison at a strip club. But Mark, a twenty-one-year-old premed student, disappeared from the street, scooped up as if by the wind, with no news of him for weeks.

Mark's parents came to Brownsville and searched for him doggedly, but information was scarce until a man speeding through a checkpoint caused officers to give chase. They found Rancho Santa Elena, where Mark had been decapitated, dismembered, and used in a ritual cauldron. He was one of more than a dozen killed by the small group of drug traffickers who subscribed to a combination of

Afro-Caribbean Palo Mayombe Santeria and Mexican witchcraft and went out one night in search of an Anglo spring breaker to sacrifice.

Pictures of Mark—with a kind, open face reminiscent of a young Matt Damon—show him with a smile so wide as to suggest a belly laugh. They're easy to find online, many posted in 2009 to mark the twentieth anniversary of his death. His parents were astonishingly graceful as the media circus swirled around them, according to a *Texas Monthly* report.

"I don't feel any anger at all, to be honest with you," James Kilroy, Mark's father, is quoted as saying, adding that he hoped the killers would apologize to his son in heaven.

When the investigation of the murders at Rancho Santa Elena was complete, the shed where the sacrifices occurred was doused in gasoline and set ablaze.

The deaths of these young men still touch a nerve in Brownsville. Some attended the same elite private school as Joey, and remember learning of his death. Others had frequented the cantinas in Matamoros that spring breakers like Mark often visited or had met Mark's grieving parents when they came to Brownsville to search for him. Maybe these deaths stuck out because of the high achievements of both young men, who excelled in academics and were close to showing how their hard work would translate in the world beyond school. Or maybe Mark's story was highlighted because I was a newcomer, and Mark, too, was from out of town.

The stories seemed to be recounted to me in an effort to convey a larger message: In Brownsville, a dissonant note troubled the warmth and community I might otherwise find, and I should be on the lookout. Violence was present, a current flowing through the city, barely visible until it hit rock and swirled into white water. Only in Brownsville, they might say as they ended such a story. *Qué* crazy.

But the story of what happened to John Allen Rubio, Angela Camacho, and the children on East Tyler Street seemed different. For one, it had been only four years since the murders when I arrived at the *Herald*. The crime was more recent, and John was waiting for his second trial, having won an appeal that showed Angela's confession had been improperly presented to the jury. The narrative had an uneasy open-endedness.

The Rubio story was also especially affecting because it concerned small children. It grabbed hold of the reporters during these newsroom conversations, the revelation of each detail making the case suddenly raw, fresh, intense. A father and a mother killing three young children—three babies!—with the crude weapon of kitchen knives. The bodies in trash bags, the heads in buckets of water, washed clean of blood. For not one but both parents to be involved in such a horror was stunning and inexplicable.

As a young reporter grappling with a place that was new to me, and which I needed to describe in print daily, I paid attention when those around me seemed to care particularly about a certain story or issue. The Rubio case also had an unusual tangibility: the filing cabinet that separated my desk from the *Herald* crime reporters' contained records from the first trial. Present, too, was the building, an ailing marker of the crime, reminding me of what had happened every time I passed by. After hearing the voices of the neighbors a hundred times as I stitched together the audio slide show in the closet-size editing suite, the case began the slow and certain process of taking up residence in my psyche.

Brownsville is not alone in its history of heinous crimes. Cities everywhere witness murders that attract parachute journalists or inspire horror films. But many of the ones that have happened here have a few common ingredients. The local culture of *curanderismo*, folk healing that is most often performed for good, and *brujería*, witchcraft that includes the casting of spells and curses, has sometimes joined the narrative. Some crimes also point to the lack of resources in Brownsville for the treatment of mental illness. Without help, unhealthy obsessions can fester, dangerous belief systems thrive, vendettas brood until such actions become, as John's attorney explained, inevitable. These murders, shocking in their retelling, must have reached that point of apparent inevitability to the killers. In their minds, at that essential moment, these actions had to be taken, whether because of delusion, honor, revenge, desperation, paranoia, or fear of an inner truth.

While I didn't come to the city to report on a murder, I soon realized how central these crimes had become to Brownsville's history, more so in the daily lives of residents than some of its proudest military victories. The restaging of the Battle of Palo Alto, the first major engagement of the Mexican-American War, by volunteers in historical dress, though also a chronicle of death, feels distant from the confrontations and struggles that shape modern lives. Yet while the battlefield has been preserved by the parks department so visitors can stand in the middle of the isolation, see the blooming cacti on the rugged plain where armies clashed, the legends of these local killings of regular people will probably not join a long-term historical narrative. Maybe they'll be used as cautionary tales to scare teenagers or other green reporters. Maybe they'll be forgotten.

On that initial visit, as I walked around the building on East Tyler Street recording audio for the slide show, my interest in the crimes was minimal. What I saw was a cheap place to live, and thus a respite for some of the city's poor. The back of the building was falling apart, an almost random arrangement of wood doors, stairs, and windows. The tenants on the second floor shared a communal bathroom, and in one apartment a woman had constructed a shrine on top of a dresser with a framed picture of the pope, candles, artificial flowers, and an image of the Virgen de Guadalupe. Brad snapped a few photographs of the doorway to the Rubio apartment, which was locked from the outside, marked with stickers as EVIDENCE.

As I put together the photos and the audio, Brad sent me a few digital images from the archives. Some were Polaroids of the children. When I looked at them, I saw happy, innocent young faces, but they remained strangers to me. Today, the images of Julissa, John Stephan, and Mary Jane are imprinted on my brain. I see them when I close my eyes. I see them when I open my eyes.

And I can see the other photograph—the one of an administrator holding up three death certificates. Each is stamped with a single assaulting word: DECEASED. DECEASED. DECEASED.

CHAPTER 3

Pilgrim

It's just a building.

—SUSAN ZAVALA, FORMER NEIGHBOR

The district clerk's office in the Cameron County Courthouse is just two blocks from the building on East Tyler and Eighth Streets in Brownsville. There, files documenting both of John's trials are kept in nineteen enormous folders and half a dozen cardboard boxes. I'd moved an hour away along the path of the river, but I'd regularly drive to Brownsville and sit in the district clerk's office in the courthouse where John was first tried, going through page after page of legal filings, with a fistful of paper clips and a peanut-butter sandwich. Sometimes freelance work would intervene and I would skip an entire week or two.

"We didn't know if you were coming back," one of the clerks would say, eyeing me curiously, before wheeling the stepladder over to the spot where they kept the Rubio files. They'd ask which of the folders I needed, and I'd go back to my usual seat, becoming another fixture in the quiet records room, listening to the pop songs

that streamed through the speakers and going through thousands of pages of bureaucratic court procedures, medical reports, and jury selection.

I didn't know quite what I was looking for at first. My hope was that the court documents would provide a logical entry point. But after a few hours, they would numb me, and I'd gather my things and visit the building before driving home. There, just two blocks away, I'd see the surrogate of my subject. The scene of the crime.

It was like the exoskeleton of a once-living thing. It had the grizzled appearance of a horror house, the kind of place ideal for ghost hunters with dubious equipment and for scaring kids around late October. The structure exuded desolation and a sleeping threat, as if it wore the face of the crime that took place inside, a seemingly perfect scapegoat.

Though 805 East Tyler stood inanimate on the corner of Eighth Street, its mortality, like John's, was at stake. I watched it the way a witness visits the bedside of a dying relative. It was there, so present and concrete. But I knew it could disappear in a moment, the bricks fired for its creation lying in a heap.

I became a pilgrim to the building—not a worshipper, but a witness. I was a disciple of the unknown lesson I believed it would teach me.

In the Library of Congress, I'd found some of the oldest remaining maps of Brownsville. The Sanborn Map Company carefully plotted out cities and towns across America, hoping to sell fire-insurance policies to local property owners. The earliest map shows a box on the street corner, etched with symbols that indicate it was a combination warehouse, grocery store, dwelling, and storage room.

That building was made of wood, one-story high, and haphazardly jumbled together.

On the 1926 map, the space that the jumble had occupied is blank. Maybe a fire had demolished the first structure. But by the 1930 map, the new building appears—a sizable two stories, part brick, part wood, with a filling station and an unusual cutout on the first floor. Here, what would have been the sharp corner of the building was flattened so cars could drive up and fill their gas tanks on the way to and from town. By the time John, Angela, and the three children moved into the apartment that occupied the spot next to that old storefront, that corner was filled in, the filling station eliminated. The family would be the apartment's last tenants.

When the building was erected, Brownsville had grown from a mud-walled army fort on the northern bank of the Rio Grande into a small city. The Fort Brown army barracks flanked the river, and New Orleans–style brick and ironwork stores shared space on the main avenues, next to the large homes of their owners. As one walked away from Mexico toward East Tyler Street, the homes diminished in size until one- and two-room houses speckled street corners near the railroad tracks. Finally, these gave way to ranchland. There, in what is today a sprawling suburban metro area, was the secluded landscape of "Lonesome Dove."

This was a large building for the neighborhood in the 1930s and was originally on Brownsville's outskirts, beyond the city plan. It occupied two full lots, stretching back from the street toward an alley behind—about 125 feet long and 50 wide. The first floor was a business and the second apartments, a detail that explains in part why the first floor was poorly arranged after it was converted into housing. Long, hallway-shaped apartments were constructed by the time the Rubio family lived here, a layout that cut the existing floor plan into strips. These apartments had doors on the street and in the back, along the grassy lot.

By 1949 the Sanborn map shows that the building was only half its original size. While it was once primarily brick with a smaller wood section in the back, the wood section was gone and only the brick remained, and it was no longer a filling station. On one of these maps the names of alleys are marked. Today these unofficial streets have no such signs to tell pedestrians or drivers their titles. But at the time the alleyways were probably the site of informal homes for the very poor, hand-me-downs of the Mexican peasants who had erected jacales, or thatched-roof huts, behind the homes of their employers. Near the railroad, it may have been a low-cost place for workers who needed a place to stay as they made their way along the line.

Another killing had taken place at this address, in the mideighties. A man caught stabbing a woman was commanded by Brownsville detective Rey Martinez to stop. When he continued to attack her, Martinez shot him, killing the man. The chief said that the woman, despite her stab wounds, miraculously lived after being rushed to the hospital with the knife still taped to her, preventing her from bleeding out.

By the 2000s, mistreatment was evident along every blemished wall and broken window of the building. Its exterior, brick long ago painted white, was the nonspecific color of filth. Wood doors with hinged screens stood apart on the first floor with no windows between them, like a prison lineup. Some of those had been boarded over with wood planks, but not the Rubio apartment.

From the front, the two-story building was severe, with a boxlike structure that suggested utility. But viewed from the back it was vulnerable, a feeble hospital patient whose disintegrating body could be undone by a gust of wind. Here, alongside the sturdy bricks, were dilapidated wood doors that no longer fit their frames. Small squares tilted to the angle of diamonds plastered near the roof, looked as if they'd been tacked on like a dutiful nod to the idea of aesthetic beauty.

Posts that once held clotheslines were scattered around the backyard. Now and then the grass was cut, but it usually grew wild and high, hiding discarded items beneath. One day I saw a child's homework, a dirty diaper, a crushed drinking cup, and a small pink plastic star. The sidewalk had split open and a rush of plump red ants poured out of their home beneath the ground. Nearby, a dead lizard was being devoured by another colony of fire ants, each the size of a grain of sand.

One of my first questions to John was whether the apartment had a window. It was hard to tell from the outside, but it appeared that their home was totally dark, with no aperture to let in light or the Gulf breeze. In the South Texas summers with no air-conditioning, the smells of cooking and children's diapers would have hung in the stagnant air.

He wrote back:

There was a small window almost to the ceiling about 4X4 inches permanently shout. And no it did not seem small or dark because we were happy just to be together and content with the little we had. We had no A/C but we would us a fan to cool us in from

31

the heat. We didn't have anything to warm us up in the winter seasons except blankets.

One photo of the crime scene showed a fan, next to the naked body of a headless child.

So only the front and back doorways could be opened. From April through October, the temperature hovers between 85 and 110 degrees during the day in South Texas.

On these slow walks around the building, I took notes on a reporter's pad, cataloging every detail, but I looked for something I knew I'd never be able to see with my eyes. It seemed as if the best way to understand the story was to go to it, to show up, to look and listen. Sometimes I'd leave feeling that I'd learned nothing, that indeed not much more was here than a structure and a bit of grass. But when I was lucky, someone would notice the woman standing with the notebook and would stop and talk to me. I'd say what I was writing about and receive instant recognition. *Los niños? Ay.* They'd inevitably have an opinion about why the crime happened. *Las drogas. La locura. La pobreza.* Drugs. Madness. Poverty. It was a brutal triumvirate. While the explanations pushed the crime into the distance and suggested that such an act couldn't happen without one or more of those components, they only drew it closer. Drugs and poverty were everywhere. Madness was another question.

• • •

John Allen Rubio
(Photo courtesy of Louie Vera)

CHAPTER 4

Letters from the Edge

I loved to see the stars.
Makes me think alot of the amazing univers we live in.
—JOHN ALLEN RUBIO

A few months after I started writing to John, he sent me a letter with a list of addresses I'd requested. They were the intersections of his childhood, the places his family lived as he was growing up. I set out on a drive around Brownsville, looking for the landscape of those early years.

Most of the locations were vague. On this street, near this school. Around this corner. I'd idle in my car and look around. On one street I'd find a white house with a collection of two dozen potted plants in the yard—a small but cheerful little home with a clean paint job and a sign, SE VENDE ÁRBOLITOS DE MANGO, NARANJA, "we sell little mango and orange trees." Then the list would lead to a run-down cream-colored apartment building with sickly green trim on a stark lot.

John could only recall leaving Brownsville on a handful of occasions. Sometimes he walked across the bridge to Matamoros, though he said this didn't really count, since everyone in Brownsville did the same. He took a school trip to San Antonio, where he ate pizza and saw the restaurants and margarita-sipping tourists flanking the city's famed River Walk. "Everything was so big and amazing to me compared to Brownsville." Once, he traveled to Arkansas to apply for a job cleaning chickens at a Tyson factory, but wrote that he failed the drug test even though he hadn't smoked marijuana in over a month. Mainly, he "stuck to my home town which I loved very much." John got to know a wide range of neighborhoods in Brownsville due to his parents' constant fights and financial instability. His family was often forced to go looking for a cheaper place to live, leaving wherever might have started to become home. John altered many details slightly as he recounted them—from statement to statement and letter to letter. I didn't always notice these variations in the moment, but taken together, they sometimes made it hard to pin down the "correct" version of events. What I have is the product of what John told me, the court record, and the results of my own inquiries.

John Allen Rubio was born on August 12, 1980, just after Hurricane Allen. His mother, Hilda, gave birth at Valley Regional Medical Center two days after Allen made landfall in Brownsville, a Category 5 storm that had simmered down to a Category 3 by the time it hit Texas. Allen knocked out power along the South Texas coast for several days, destroyed half of the region's cotton and citrus crops, and left residents without drinking water.

Hilda was in her early twenties when she gave birth to John and already had another son, Manuel, with a different man. Soon, two more brothers, Rodrigo and Jose Luis, would join the bunch. Hilda came from a large family herself—she was one of twelve children, six boys and six girls. Her own mother, Felicitas, would have forty-one grandchildren by the time she died.

John lived in several different neighborhoods spread across Brownsville, such as Cameron Park, a *colonia* that, while technically within the city limits, isn't part of Brownsville proper. For a time he lived at his grandparents' house in Barrio Buena Vida. He also lived in Southmost, a neighborhood close to the outer limits of Brownsville and the Rio Grande. There, the orange groves, cornfields, and nature sanctuary shared space along the river's snaking path. Turning down one street in this neighborhood led to a pocket of houses and parks. Turning down another, the levee appeared, where green Border Patrol trucks kicked up dust along the edge of the United States.

John's second letter described his time growing up in Brownsville, his "poor, disfuntional family," and the beatings his mother frequently endured.

It was six of us living in the same house. My mom, my dad, my older half brother, myself, and two younger brothers. All us kids slept in the same bed most of the time except when we were kids and our parents bought us two bunk beds, one for each of us. We all slept in the same room always because we would get small places to live.

As a child I imagened myself living in a house built just for me. My perfect wife and perfect kids. I always wanted to be in the milatery so I thought this dream would come through some day and even promised my mother that some day I would make her a house right next to my own so I can have her close to me forever. Growing up I loved both my parents but I was closer to my mom because she showed interesse in the things I did and liked. At least that was the way things were until she started doing crack cocain and changed alot.

I wanted to stay in Brownsville but buy a peace of land unde-veloped where there is not much people or houses so it could be quiet. Enjoy the trees, animals that run around grassy places and the stars. I loved to see the stars. Makes me think alot of the amaz-ing univers we live in.

Hilda testified that John's father beat her so badly, sometimes she couldn't open her eyes, and her older brother Juan said that both John and Hilda were beaten. "He used to just throw him all over the place, like if nothing mattered." Juan told defense attorney Nat Perez Jr. that he wished he had reported the abuse to police, but didn't because "we were going to take care of it ourselves." Hilda said John's father merely spanked him, but said that he did start giving John alcohol as early as age five, when he would feed the kindergartener beer.

"My father was very abusive, psysically, emotionally and men-tally," John wrote. "He seemed to struggle with expressing and/or excepting love."

The mitigation phase, during which his attorneys tried to show how difficult John's life had been and give the jury a reason to spare him the death penalty, put his family in a harsh light. As John was sentenced during the second trial, neither Hilda nor his brothers came to support him.

I drove by one home near Porter High School, where John grad-uated in 1999, when he was almost nineteen. He remembered an exact address. The house was painted blue, with white bars over the windows and the door, and was surrounded by a large green lot. It didn't have the claustrophobic feeling of the apartment that would be John's final home before prison. Here the boys could have played together, kicking a soccer ball through the grass, not unlike the children a mile away, in backyards abutting resacas. They might have watched some of John's favorite movies—*The Wizard of Oz*, *Grease*, *The Sound of Music*, and *Mary Poppins*. John remembered playing video games as a kid, one of his favorite activities. Sometimes, he played a cowboy game his father found at a flea market. He also liked catching tarantulas.

In one of his letters, John described his rivalry with his brother Jose Luis:

> I was very wild, climing trees, running around, playing all kinds of crazy games and my little brothers would follow me around because I would do fun stuff. Rodrigo was more garded, to himself but let go when we were playing. He took things seriously. Jose Luis as like my arc-enemy, or so he thought I was his. He would always be looking to get me angry with him. He would lye in wait for me, hit me and then run to our parents yelling at the top of his head "Juan [John in Spanish] wants to hit me for no reason." Really, for no reason!!! He was such a big lier an acter that my parents always believed him and it did not help that he was the baby of the house.

During the second trial, defense attorney Perez confronted Hilda with prior testimony that she had used crack cocaine while pregnant with John, but Hilda was adamant that she had not. She did admit to drinking a six-pack of beer a day all nine months, despite having been told that she shouldn't drink while pregnant. Her brother Juan testified that he saw Hilda huff paint during the pregnancy.

Dr. Jolie S. Brams, a psychologist who testified at the second trial, said John likely had a thought disorder as early as preschool, and his ability to distinguish between reality and fantasy was impaired. Dr. Brams found John's parents to have had a "toxic" influence, "whose negativity and their behavior and their dysfunction in their daily lives hampered John Rubio's ability to be a normal healthy individual."

John struggled with language as a child. Dr. Brams said he was unable to speak English fluently and "would talk to things that weren't there. But even when he spoke to his family members, he kind of did it in his own gibberish, as if he were living in his own world." His motor skills were also delayed—he never crawled and walked late. He had night terrors and believed in witchcraft. These, Dr. Brams said, were early "seeds of psychosis." Dr. Brams concluded that John's difficult upbringing exacerbated his developmental problems.

But young John loved Hilda and clung to her, and his recollections in letters were of a mother in whom he could confide, who cared about his problems. He loved her more than anyone else and described her as a "best friend, a father and a mother, a counselor." His uncle Juan described her as a good mother who loved her children and worked hard to support them for many years, until "the picture turned around."

"You know, it's like when you look in the mirror and you see yourself, all of the sudden you just grab the image that's inside and bring it out, and that's the opposite side of you? That's what happened to her."

An ex-boyfriend of Hilda's, who met her while she was working as a nursing assistant in the nineties, said Hilda quit her job after several steady years, telling him that "she was tired." It seems that after this point, her substance abuse problem worsened.

When I asked John for good memories of his childhood, he told me this story twice: His special-education class was putting on a performance, and the children were to pretend they were playing paper instruments while music swelled in the background from the stereo.

I needed white gloves, white button shirt, and black slacks. My father thought it was stupid but my mother thought it would be good for me to gain confidence so she bought me what I needed and because my dad didn't want to drive us to school, my mother and I walked the 2 miles or so to the school.

John was handed a cardboard saxophone, he recalled, and pretended it was real as the tape played behind them.

I was full of childish joy and loved the fact my mother didn't just get the things I needed but came with me all the way to school. My dad really did think it was stupid but because my mother saw it was important to me it did not matter if it was stupid or not, she just wanted to give me a little happyness.

Hilda recalled throwing John birthday parties every year, buying piñatas and having his friends over, but John's brothers remembered a different Hilda when they were on the witness stand. At John's ROTC parades, Hilda was absent. The four brothers shared a single bedroom and woke most mornings to find Hilda passed out from drinking. They had to dress John and make sure he tied his shoes before school, something they said he sometimes had trouble doing even in high school. Manuel, the oldest, would cook for the boys when he was home, but once he moved out, they often had to fend for themselves, eating whatever was around. John's younger brother Rodrigo remembered getting a book as a gift for Christmas one year, and a Tonka toy. Those are the only Christmas presents he ever recalled receiving from Hilda. John's uncle Juan painted an even bleaker picture, based on the time he lived with them: John went to school wearing dirty clothes, birthdays were not celebrated, and as for Christmas, "We had no Christmas tree, we had no presents, we had nothing."

Brownsville has ranked several times as the poorest city in the United States. As of the most recent census, more than a third of its residents lived below the poverty level, with a population that was 93 percent Hispanic, the vast majority of Mexican descent. The region's institutions of higher education have historically been underfunded by legislators in Austin. There is no law school here, or for 250 miles within the United States, and only after decades of battles has a medical school at last been planned. As an outgrowth of this, the region has lacked doctors who specialize in mental health. To become a professional in medicine or law, the best and brightest have continuously been drawn far away. If they stay in Brownsville, they often find that they cannot realize their aspirations because the tools to do so are simply nonexistent.

In a city of such overwhelming poverty, John and his brothers' lives may not have been so unique. Many families struggled to feed their children, and getting government lunches at school was not the exception but the norm. Parents worked late hours or lived in Mexico and sent their children to live with a relative, so a lack of homework help wasn't unusual. In one way, such children might have seen themselves as fortunate: they weren't among their classmates who had just crossed *la frontera* from Mexico and spoke no English.

I met one of John's teachers from elementary school, Pablo Coronado Jr. When he'd heard about the case on the news, more than a decade after John left his classroom, he didn't immediately recognize his former student. Then it clicked: he had been a silly little boy in his class during one of his first years as a teacher. John, he remembered, always tried to make his classmates laugh.

Coronado remembered John as a child who was in need of care, whose clothes were often dirty. Sadly, Coronado said, his situation was not unheard of, even in the second grade.

"They come with a lot of baggage already," he said. Coronado remembered that he tried to begin the process of getting John extra help. He requested a psychological evaluation. In third grade, John was diagnosed as emotionally disturbed and Hilda said John told her he was seeing shadows. She reported this to the Social Security office.

When John heard or saw something strange, he told me that he would ask the person next to him if he or she did, too. Sometimes people said they had. He took such occasions as evidence that unusual forces were in the world that other people were also at a loss to explain. Hilda corroborated this in her testimony, saying that John told her he was the chosen one, but that she didn't see this as a cause for concern.

Dr. Brams believed Hilda didn't handle John's delusions appropriately: "One of the issues here is that children will become what their parents help them become. And I know that may sound trite, but that's very true." Hilda and John had a love-hate relationship, according to Dr. Brams's analysis. "She rejected him but she also manipulated him. And one way that she did that was by convincing him that witchcraft was real and demons were real and that these spirits might really exist. And instead of what a good parent would do—'Look, John, these things are not real, and I'm going to help you and comfort and support you'—she encouraged him to believe that those apparitions, those delusions, had some substance."

Juan remembered John saying that he was going to destroy the devil. When asked in court why he didn't tell Hilda, Juan said, "I wasn't going to snitch on him on his mother."

John mailed me copies of some of his school reports from his elementary days through high school. In his request for a psychological evaluation, Coronado wrote that eight-year-old John required "constant attention in class in order for him to complete assignments." He also exhibited low self-esteem.

> John is not motivated by rewards offered for completed work or good behavior. He seeks approval and acceptance by his peers but their interactions with him are often limited. Peers tend to avoid interactions with him. He often feels that no one cares.

On the same form, below the question "What is the problem as the mother sees it?," Hilda's take is that "he is just spoiled." His father noted John's mood swings: "He can be happy one minute and unhappy the next." Juan also told me that John would get angry when he didn't get his way. The same year, his teacher reported that John had thoughts that were inappropriate to a given situation, and that his behavior could be "self-serving" and "manipulative." He lacked social awareness and could act in ways that were "idiosyncratic" and "bizarre." Young John was already found to show signs of pervasive depression, a term the teacher underlined.

Coronado said that John seemed like he had potential, but the support wasn't there in his home life to help him realize it.

At age ten, John's learning abilities seemed to be improving. His special-education teacher wrote that John "has made huge strides in reading this year," "uses fluent English," though he did not always use correct grammar, and had excellent math and science skills. But at the end of an otherwise positive report, the teacher wrote that John was a "very emotionally needy child—he often reverts to babyish behavior as a coping or attention getting behavior. Parents should be encouraged to do parent training classes. (This has not happened so far)."

The following year, a teacher noted he had "little patience, he calls out, he gets upset when someone says anything mean or upsetting to him. He has trouble ignoring."

The checks to support John's disability helped keep the family afloat. John told me that Hilda used them to pay the rent, and she sold food stamps to pay utility bills.

In sixth grade his emotionally disturbed label was removed after he took behavioral improvement classes.

John couldn't remember his exact age when his parents split for good, but it was around his fourteenth year. In the past, Hilda had broken up with her husband after a particularly bad brawl, only to get back together. This time it was permanent. When John's father came to visit, he took John to a bar and bought him a beer. John remembered waking up the next day to screaming.

JOHN! JOHN!

His mother was yelling for him to come help her, he wrote: His father had stayed the night, too drunk to drive home, and Hilda needed John's help to protect her from him. John said he asked his father to sleep it off or leave.

> He told me he was my dad, that he tells me what to do NOT the other way around. I told him the same thing again and he slapped me. When he slapped me in my mind I saw ALL the times he beat up on my mom, how he would tell me I was worthless and always would be worthless, and lots of other things he would say and do that were really hurtful, and I put all that hurt and anger into a punch that hit him right in the face and I knocked him out.

John went outside with his two brothers. When they came back, their father was gone.

> My mom would pick guys ever since that would hit her and I'd defend her from about 4 of her boyfriends. But my father I rarely saw except those 5 times within 8 or 9 years from when they separated until I got arrested for this.

Hilda's sister Genoveva Ramirez testified that there was a sudden change in her behavior. She'd been a good mother, a provider, and then "she just turned around and went for the worst." John's brother remembered Hilda's calling John *mongolo* as a child, a slang word equivalent to "retard." Dr. Brams found that the more John clung to Hilda, the more she rejected him. John remembered that Hilda's "most important priority was crack."

During John's high school years, he found some companionship

and purpose in extracurricular activities. He had a talent for dancing and participated in parades during Charro Days, doing tradi-
tional Mexican folk dances with his classmates, and Juan said John's
abilities stood out. He also performed choreographed dances with
a group of about six other teens at neighborhood parties, including the elaborate birthday parties for fifteen-year-old girls called
quinceañeras. Memorizing the steps required intense concentration. John remembered performing almost every week, sometimes
multiple events in the same weekend. He did backflips; he liked the
challenge and the attention they brought. The dancers would split
the money they received.

John was then on the swim team and in the ROTC, or Reserve
Officers' Training Corps, as well. As a kid who was always different—in special classes, struggling with behavioral problems—he'd
found a couple of spaces where he could belong, wearing the same
uniform as his classmates, and was given positive reinforcement.
The ROTC meant even more than that—it was a gateway to joining
the military and therefore resolved the question of what John would
do once school ended.

His swim coach, Luis Ortega, still worked at Porter High School
when I contacted him. He'd been there since 1979. With his clear
and intentional responses to my questions, it was easy to imagine
him teaching Advanced Placement government classes, as he did
when he wasn't coaching. He punctuated pauses with a question of
his own—Am I making sense?—the refrain of a teacher determined
to keep his students engaged.

Ortega told me that many students didn't know how to swim
when they joined the team, and everyone who did join was provided

with a uniform, cap, goggles, bag, and a warm-up suit, free of charge. Though John wasn't on an especially winning team, he made a lasting impression on Ortega as a diligent teammate who led workouts and dependably showed up for practice. He wasn't particularly tall, but Ortega called the good-looking, fit young man Big John, to mentally build him up. After his having been called many variations of "stupid" at home, it's easy to imagine how much this must have meant to him.

"He wasn't a troublemaker. He wasn't a kid we could say had major issues, at least I didn't see that," Ortega said. "He was a kid that was very much involved in taking care of his image; he was always in great shape. He worked hard in the water. He wasn't the greatest of swimmers at all, but one of the better kids that we had in terms of being committed to what we did, working out, never complained, did everything we asked."

Ortega said that it was almost more common for students at the school to be poor, to struggle outside of Porter's walls, than not. The swim team, like the basketball or football team, served many functions for the athletes. It was a way to avoid neighborhood gangs and other truant behavior. The swimmers were so exhausted after a day of school and laps, they had no energy to search out the influences that got their peers into trouble. In this way, Ortega saw himself as providing more than swimming lessons or fitness for the students.

Today, Porter is a magnet school, known for its engineering program. The population has changed slightly, as Brownsville has become a bigger city, and the school has larger and better facilities than when John was attending. But it's still located in the poor Southmost neighborhood, and many students continue to fend off local gangs and drugs in an effort to make better lives for themselves. Porter has always had successful students, too, who have gone on to the Ivy League and high achievement. It's frustrating for Ortega and his fellow teachers whenever an article in the *Herald* indicates that a recent crime was committed by a "former Porter student."

"We at Porter have not lost that essence of what we're supposed to be doing for these kids: giving them the sense of belonging, even though they don't have it at home."

The school responds to the emotional need that students have to belong to a community, as well as addressing survival requirements that are far more basic.

"They come and eat breakfast and lunch, and most of them don't have dinner at home," Ortega said. "Some kids can't get out of wherever they live because it rains and they're flooded in. It's cold, it's warm at school. It's hot, it's cool at school."

When he saw the headlines about such students, he thought "that we failed them. That we failed them. Somehow, we didn't get to them," Ortega told me. "It hurts to a certain degree because we were not able to put them in the right direction, because he did what he did."

While at Porter, John appeared for his first couple of years to have had his life on track, although he faced some challenges. In the school library I looked at yearbooks of the mid-to-late nineties, when John attended, but found few pictures of him. In one, he was lined up with the rest of the students in the ROTC. In a solo portrait, he was smiling, relaxed, with thick black hair and the barely visible mustache of a kid who hasn't yet begun to shave.

Though John said it wasn't until around age twenty that he first engaged in prostitution, Dr. Brams concluded that Hilda pushed him into these activities at around age twelve. Until his arrest, John had both male and female lovers. Jose Angel Nuñez Jr., part of the dance troupe, was one such partner. John wrote to me about Jose Angel.

> He said that I would never do this as there was nothing that I ever wanted was to be a father. He knew this because we had spent alot of time talking about what we each wanted out of life. I was only 16 years old but wanted to be loved and love a family of my own. That is why he said that about me. His additude was very similar to Angelas which is why I think they got along so well that first time they met. I believe he only came one more time and they still got along great. Even so I would not leave Angela and my kids for anyone.

When he testified, Jose Angel remembered two sides of John—a young man who seemed, most of the time, to be engaged in normal teenage activities like dancing and going to the movies—but who also acted oddly, sometimes getting up in the night to talk to his grandmother, who wasn't there, as he rocked back and forth. John believed his grandmother to be a witch, or *bruja*, and Jose Angel said, that was his "whole world." John's grandmother had died in 1994. She had a collection of troll dolls, which Hilda called a hobby, but John saw as something more sinister. His brother Manuel described her at trial as someone a small child would realistically find frightening. "She looked like a witch," he testified. "Puffy hair, long hair, long nails." About three inches long, he said, and John wrote to me that they were curled like claws. Rodrigo said he avoided talking to her because she scared him. "She was always being really mean to everyone."

But their uncle Juan insisted that she was not a witch. She may have taken them to *curanderas* as kids or had some religious objects in her home, but she was not practicing black witchcraft, he said.

"She was the mayonnaise of the family," Juan said. "She was the one that binded everything together."

In 1997, when John was a high school junior, he met Georgina Castillo, Jose Angel Nuñez's cousin, who was known as Gina. She was about ten years older than John, with two young kids of her own. Gina and John began having sex every few weeks, he told detectives, and she tried to give him money afterward.

"I was like, 'No, I don't want no money, I feel like you're paying for it,' you know. She said, 'No, accept it. I know you need the help.'" On the witness stand, Gina told the court that she never paid him for sex, and the insinuation was upsetting.

Gina, John said, got him to quit the dance group, out of jealousy. "Even if I wasn't flirting with them, a girl would be flirting with me," John asserted. For a time John and Gina lived with Hilda, and then they moved into a place of their own. John felt he'd found real love. Defense attorney Perez, who served as cocounsel for John at both trials, said that Gina was a mother figure for John.

"He has somebody that loves him, somebody that cuddles him, somebody that makes him breakfast," Perez said. But there was a problem. "Gina was looking for a boyfriend, somebody that, as a man, was going to pull his weight. And like she clearly said to me, it was like having a third child."

Gina said that John would spend the day playing video games while she worked two jobs and cooked the family's meals. She claimed to have banished John from the kitchen because she was afraid he'd burn himself.

Gina also remembered John's being fixated on his grandmother. When he told her about these episodes, he'd cry nervously. John wrote to me that he had never been close to his grandmother in real life, but that she often played a part in his dreams.

Q. Was there an occasion that John told you about a vision that he had?

A. On one occasion he was asleep, he was asleep and I woke him up, and he was frightened.

Q. And what was it that John told you?

A. That his grandmother who did not leave him alone, and that he would be the chosen one to continue with whatever she had been doing.

John's eleventh-grade special-education case manager was Delfina Treviño, a woman he sometimes called Mom. Delfina remembered John as respectful, well behaved, and high functioning compared to her other students, some of whom couldn't read or write. Delfina wrote in John's report that year that he was hyperactive and liked "to goof off." "He will ask his regular teachers permission to go to content mastery then spend the time roaming the halls, talking to different people."

By 1999, at age eighteen, John was living with Gina and her kids. A school report indicated that his emotional troubles hadn't disappeared and may have been worsening.

John has had trouble in some of his classes. His teachers [ROTC] reports that his lack of discipline led to his termination in the

ROTC program. His inappropriate behavior on the access of the internet led him to be barred from using the internet through BISD [Brownsville Independent School District] equipment. He has had excessive absences and is aware of his need to appeal for credit."

By the twelfth grade, John was reading and doing math on a fourth-grade level, but he graduated anyway.

At the end of high school, John recalled setting out to accomplish his dream of joining the military. It was before 9/11, and he didn't have a cause in mind. "I wanted to be all that I could be," he told me, inspired by the army slogan. A military career could have helped John realize his goals: buying a house, creating a family with Gina, and providing for them. Maybe his mother would turn her life around and spend time with them, nurturing grandkids the way he remembered her doing for him and his brothers early in their childhood. He hoped to build something permanent, something no landlord could take away. It was at around that time that John's grandparents' house burned down, where he had lived before moving out with Gina and her kids. "My diploma, clothes, and everything burned down with the house," he wrote.

In letters, John told me that he attempted to apply to join the army and then the marines, but failed the required aptitude test several times. Physically, he said he was capable, but he couldn't pass the written exam. John had dreamed about joining the military since he was a kid, watching G.I. Joe cartoons. Now, that dream was finished.

After about two years together, Gina broke off the relationship. She was frustrated, she testified, that John would spend the whole day at home, doing nothing but playing video games. John was devastated. He'd smoked pot for fun in high school, but now he was smoking to forget and dull the pain of heartbreak. He moved back in with Hilda, along with Jose Luis, Rodrigo, and his wife. Sometimes Hilda would buy him pot, saying it was a protective measure: she would interface with drug dealers so John wouldn't have to.

Sometimes, John recreationally took rufilin, the date-rape drug, which he called roach pills. "They made me blackout and violet," he wrote. Usually he huffed paint, a cheap high that resulted in a fleeting euphoria and dizziness. He'd been huffing since he was a teenager and told a court-appointed psychiatrist that he rarely went three or four days without using spray. John recalled that inhaling the fumes made his thoughts come faster. "I felt more like the real me, or like I used to feel when I was a kid alive and active," he wrote. "It was like my mind was a clogged up drain and the spray was draino so the thoughts came easyer and more automatic." He stopped using spray and other drugs for a time. He was subjected to drug testing while on probation for possession of marijuana, and he also submitted to testing to get the kids back after Child Protective Services intervened. Still, it seemed that the urge to self-medicate, or simply addiction, never disappeared.

Angela hated for me to do spray paint. She told me contless times that she would rather I smoke weed than do spray paint. She and I had never fought over anything else except twice for this in the almost 3 years we were together. I wanted to make her happy but found myself craving the sansation the spray gave me so after about 2 or 3 months of not doing any I would fall off the wagen as they say for about 2 weeks or so.

After high school, John had intermittent jobs at fast-food restaurants and considered himself good at fixing things, but without his goal of joining the military, he lacked direction. The drugs were also taking a serious toll on his brain, as his IQ dropped from a childhood score upwards of 90, close to average, to 72 by the time he was twenty-three.

At that time, John and Angela were living in the same apartment complex, and John saw that Angela was being abused by her boyfriend.

"I used to say that reminds me of when my ex used to treat me that way. I said, if I had a woman like that, I would not treat her that way," he told detectives. "I would make her happy until the last moment of my life. Until the day I die, I would make her happy."

Angela and Julissa came to live with John, Hilda, and his brothers. It was crowded, and they would soon move out on their own.

In some cities the threat of violence is open. In Caracas, Venezuela, a city with one of the highest murder rates in the world, I remember the visceral chill that went through me when I realized the sun had gone down and I would have to walk the half mile back to the apartment where I was staying. It was tragic to see the orange blush of the sky and feel the cool mountain air and find yourself filled with dread. I've never felt this kind of fear in Brownsville. The violence here is mainly shuttered inside homes or waiting on the banks of the Rio Grande when drug loads are dropped. The police logs are filled with intimate crimes, and while random theft and acts of violence do occur, domestic abuse and drug-related crime is far more common. When someone is killed seemingly at random, most people assume he or she knew the wrong people, was involved in the wrong thing. If you kept to yourself, to people you trusted, you'd be safe.

As I drove around looking for the remains of John's childhood, it felt both accessible and cordoned off. True comprehension was a moving target. New details invited new questions, some impossible to answer. What does it feel like to have your own mother say that prostitution is a viable option? What would compel a person to voluntarily and repeatedly take a drug that others use to facilitate the rape of unsuspecting victims?

I'd gone looking for Hilda several times, once with Manuel, the nephew of Minerva Perez, one of the building's neighbors. They both knew Hilda and had many friends in the neighborhood. Conversations with residents across Barrio Buena Vida led us to her little apartment on a street corner. After several attempts we found her at home, and she told Manuel she would talk with me another day. But when I followed up, she didn't answer the door, and eventually I found a note written in large letters on a piece of cardboard—a declaration to leave her alone. I obeyed. John's brothers refused to speak with me, saying through a relative that the experience was still too painful. I left them notes at every address and business I could find in Brownsville that was linked to them and contacted them online, but when I continued to be refused, I left it alone. So much had been said during the trials, a history of abuse, sorrow, regret. They'd endured cameras, the rejection of their community, in addition to living through the death of their nieces and nephew. I knew I would never understand what they'd endured. The sadness here was suffocating, a tidal wave that threatened to crush all in its path, then pull the wreckage out to sea.

CHAPTER 5

The Long Shadow of Small Ghosts

I miss them dearly. I need them so much.
—ANGELA SALDIVAR, GRANDMOTHER

In the court file are copies of the children's medical records. At two years and three months, Julissa was taken to the Brownsville Kiddie Health Center and found to be dirty, her feet black, clothes smelly, and her skin covered with scars from insect bites. She was anemic and prescribed iron. The assessment read "child neglect." At four months old, John Stephan was also found to be filthy, his skin crusty and oily, his clothes smelling of mildew. His eyes were mildly sunken and he was in the third percentile for height, fifth for weight. The same month, a report had been filed with Child Protective Services alleging that the children were malnourished, anemic, covered in mosquito bites, and that John was likely using drugs. John recalled that the family had been homeless, often sleeping on a mattress in an alley or an abandoned building during that period. A CPS worker would testify that the family was found to be staying in a one-bedroom apartment with no electricity or running water, and no food. Though the children were anemic and had not received immunizations, they were not found to be malnourished.

A CPS caseworker came to visit the family and observed men who were visibly intoxicated around the children, though Angela was not on drugs herself. Rather than having the children forcibly removed, Angela decided to bring them to Los Fresnos to live with her mother. Since John was not the biological father of Julissa or John Stephan, the decision was hers to make. John was arrested for possession of marijuana close to that time, but his sentence was suspended and he was put on probation.

The family usually ate their meals at the Good Neighbor Settlement House, a soup kitchen in Barrio Buena Vida that supplies three meals a day, clothes, and showers to the needy. The spare, cinderblock cafeteria is full most every day. During the week, when the older kids are at school, adults dominate the room. They're a mixture of homeless and low-income people trying to supplement food stamps. John and Angela's children never made it to school; they were too young. The family was a fixture at Good Neighbor, located conveniently a few blocks away. Along with the Boys and Girls Club, it was the children's main point of contact with the rest of the city.

In May of 2003, just two months after the crimes occurred, the University of Texas at Brownsville and Texas Southmost College published a report about Barrio Buena Vida. Though the researchers tried to highlight the area's assets, like its central location and walkability, they also included some disturbing data about violent crime from the previous few years. In 2002, 91 percent of all reported rapes in the city happened in this neighborhood, a small section of the city that was home to just 2.1 percent of its population. Nine percent of aggravated assaults and 7 percent of robberies occurred there as well.

The Brownsville Herald is located here, as well, and I'd often pass Good Neighbor on my way to work. The friendly-looking center had a cubist mural with two women's faces painted on the far wall. The whole complex was surrounded by a high chain-link fence.

It was the children who led me back to Good Neighbor. They were the victims at the center of the crime, but I knew just a few scattered details about each of them. I struggled to glimpse a fragment of their identities. I wondered what made them laugh, if they were friendly to other children, what games they played with each other, what their voices sounded like. I wondered how the precariousness of their living situation affected them. In a way I was searching for the DNA of whom they would have become. A colleague I told about the story remarked that children can weather tough situations, playing with whatever's available. I wanted to believe that. John's assessment that the family was "happy just to be together and content with the little we had" was also a comforting fantasy. But I'd studied the catastrophic ways childhood trauma can impact people for life. In the Adverse Childhood Experiences (ACE) Study, Dr. Robert Anda from the Centers for Disease Control and Prevention and Dr. Vincent Felitti from Kaiser Permanente tracked a group of more than seventeen thousand adults, mostly middle- and upper-class white San Diegans, and found that adverse experiences during their early years had a major impact on their physical and mental health later in life. There was a direct correlation between the number of ACEs they'd had and their likelihood to suffer from depression, addictive behaviors, heart disease, cancer, and early death. In his book *How*

Children Succeed: Grit, Curiosity, and the Hidden Power of Character, journalist Paul Tough writes about the resilience it takes for children to overcome this early adversity, observing that it is just one in a set of noncognitive skills needed to achieve success. Though many children face the same obstacles, some are able to rise above while others are not. Their relationship with their parents is an especially important predictor of which group they will fall into. Is there a sense of empathic understanding or indifference? Is there safety, or the stress that comes with uncertainty? The love that Angela and John showed the children was important, but the idea that Mary Jane, John Stephan, and Julissa were happily gliding through the chaos that surrounded them was suspect. John blamed his problems on his dysfunctional childhood, then insisted that his own kids were perfectly happy even when they were sometimes homeless, and their father was doing drugs, working as a prostitute, and suffering from mental-health issues that likely extended to schizophrenia.

There was no evidence that John or Angela abused the children before the crimes, but scenes such as one in neighbor Nydia Hernandez's statement to police about an incident two weeks prior to the murders added to a concerning portrait:

"I saw the male subject and the female subject together and they had one of the children in the stroller. The male subject allowed the stroller (with the child in it) to go and it rolled down the sidewalk and it slammed into my truck. The child who was in the stroller started to cry. Neither one of the subjects did anything. All that the male subject did was pull the stroller back."

I found a few images of the children online and in the court record. A Polaroid shows John Stephan sitting on the floor in diapers, with aviator sunglasses and an oversize cross around his neck, a sly smile on his face like a baby Hells Angel. In a photo of John Stephan and another little boy, John Stephan is wearing a blue-and-yellow-striped polo shirt, a tiny pair of jeans, and sneakers, and he gazes up at the camera with a tuft of dark hair swept across his forehead. In the several photos of Julissa at various ages of toddlerhood, she has curly jet-black hair, sometimes pulled into pigtails. In one, she is smiling fiercely, all her teeth bared. In another, she is snuggled with John and John Stephan on a bed, with a soft, close-lipped grin. In the only image of Mary Jane, a healthy and happy-looking John is holding her up for the camera, bursting with paternal pride. She's tiny and wears a red-and-blue onesie and looks up and to the left, her soft, toothless mouth open and her tongue sitting near her lips.

One day, when I was trying to find neighbors willing to be interviewed, a young woman with bright-pink lipstick wearing a pink silk blouse and daisy dukes approached me. She looked as if she'd stepped out of a photo shoot. Her car was idling by the curb while she glanced anxiously at the house I was approaching. She was waiting for her boyfriend, she said, and he was at his grandmother's house. She wanted to know if I would knock on the door because his grandmother intimidated her. Dogs were in the yard and I paused. Maybe we could call him? She asked if she could borrow my phone. A couple minutes later Miguel Angel Ramos, tall and lanky, walked out of his grandmother's house and onto the curb.

"She's writing about that family in that building," the girlfriend told him. Then to me: "He knew them, he used to tell me about it. He used to play with the kids."

Miguel Angel's eyes grazed the building, as if he could see the family walking around the corner. "I used to play with them on the basketball court when they were little. The mom and dad were always at the crack houses."

Miguel Angel told me that John and Angela would often leave Julissa and John Stephan at the Boys and Girls Club, catty-corner to the apartment building. The children, just toddlers, would play for a while with the other neighborhood kids, their unchanged diapers weighed down, and then, as if an inaudible whistle had blown, they'd return home.

Miguel Angel was young when the murders happened—around eleven years old. It's easy to imagine him wading deeper and deeper into the mythology of the murders like a character in *The Goonies*. Across the street, there was a family with fourteen children. Miguel Angel said he and his friends called them Los Hernandez, like a gang. That's whom Miguel Angel hung out with, along with the little kids from the Rubio building.

Then, on March 11, cop cars swarmed the street. The area was barricaded and the apartment cordoned off as evidence. When the police departed, Miguel Angel remembered going into the apartment and seeing the blood on the floor, the porn magazines. He even said that he had had a confrontation with John the day before the murders. John, Miguel Angel said, was standing on the sidewalk, hitting little John Stephan. Miguel Angel's friends, a few of the Los Hernandez siblings, told John they were going to call Child Protective Services. According to Miguel Angel, John said he didn't care if they called CPS. Miguel Angel said that a friend of his did, indeed, make a call, but that the children were dead the next day. I asked Miguel Angel why he wasn't subpoenaed, why no one had heard this perhaps crucial piece of information during either of the trials.

"We were always out there," Miguel Angel said, indicating the corner where the neighborhood kids used to hang out across from the building. "They didn't even ask us any questions. They just told everyone to clear out."

I found an article in *The Houston Chronicle* quoting a Maria Hernandez, mother of fourteen, who told the paper she had called the Brownsville Police Department shortly before the murders and reported that people in the apartment were using drugs.

"They never listened when I made the call," she told the *Chronicle*. "It didn't have to happen."

In the article, Police Chief Carlos Garcia said the department did get a call about the apartment. "But with those kinds of calls, you have to corroborate the information. We consider it intelligence," he said. "You don't just go and knock on people's doors and violate their rights. Even if we had followed up on this information, that doesn't mean these killings wouldn't have happened."

Miguel Angel still kept watch on the building when he came to Brownsville and noted the changes. Even with my regular pilgrimages, I'd failed to notice a new fan in a second-floor window, above the Rubio apartment.

"Someone's living in there," he said.

His girlfriend had heard the stories many times. The tale of the crimes had become part of Miguel Angel's story. He looked over the evidence like a kid detective; through that final confrontation with John, he was linked to the day the crimes took place.

An intangible echo of the children's essence began to manifest through Miguel Angel's stories. They were like shadows to me now: long and inexact and opaque, but a whisper more than nothing.

At Good Neighbor, a couple of toddlers were eating lunch. One had curly hair, one straight. Their young mother scooped them up soon after I sat down at their table, along with slices of bread and cookies folded into napkins, taken home for later. Sister Luz Cardenas testified that she often saw John, Angela, and the children at Good Neighbor. John was always polite, she told the court, and would compliment the food. He was gentle with the children, serving them before he served himself. Angela, she said, was usually quiet.

Within a few minutes I was asked if I was married by a large, sweaty man with a dead front tooth and was told a series of incoherent conspiracy theories by a kind-faced former scientist in need of psychiatric medication. The latter presented me a manila envelope full of papers and told me we were going to write a Nobel Prize–winning article together. Two of the documents were apparently from government entities in Switzerland and Mexico. One letter thanked the man for his paper and stated that it had indeed been accepted for a 1978 conference in Zurich. One sheet listed random names and phrases: Leon Panetta; Nikola Tesla; Cure for Cancer; Michael Faraday; Elixer; $93 Billion (ESCROW). He read these off to me as if they were part of a coherent whole. I told him I had to go, that I had a meeting, but he insisted that we make copies in the front office.

As I walked out to my car, the director of Good Neighbor approached me. I asked him if he knew anything about the scientist's backstory.

"He showed us some pictures where he was in a classroom setting and of course he was much younger, and it looked like he was lecturing, and from what I understand at one time he was a very bright, very intelligent guy."

"I believe it."

"He has a lot of knowledge up there."

"So what do you do for someone like that? I mean, is there anything you can do, or do you just help him when he comes in?"

"There really isn't much we can do. He doesn't want to be helped. He'll want to call up the president. . . . He calls a lot of people."

I went back to Good Neighbor to check out a crafts class, where a group of women were given free materials, with the goal of helping them make a profit from their crafts and create a self-sustaining enterprise. That week, in preparation for Thanksgiving, they were using ribbon, thread, and hot glue guns to make turkey pins. The tail feathers were yellow, and the turkeys, with googly eyes, had little orange feet hanging down at the bottom. A petite, enthusiastic woman from Matamoros had started the class two years earlier. She'd come to Good Neighbor to spread God's word, but realized that the soup kitchen's patrons also needed a way to make money. She changed the arrangement, teaching one hour of art, one hour of Bible study each week. After the turkey pins were done, a plain-looking woman who had formerly said little took charge of a microphone attached to a karaoke machine.

She spoke excitedly about passages from the Bible. *"Lo que Dios dice, se cumple."* What God says, he does.

The two dozen women in the room joined in on the *se cumple*.

On Rosh Hashanah, the Jewish New Year, I'd sat in a synagogue listening to a reform rabbi deliver his sermon about a familiar passage in the Torah: the story of Abraham and Isaac. God orders Abraham to sacrifice his son Isaac, and Abraham endeavors to comply with God's command. But just before the moment of sacrifice, God sends an angel to Abraham to grant Isaac a reprieve. Instead, Abraham sacrifices a ram, and father and son return safely home together.

Many of the stories in the Torah drift away, but that of Abraham and Isaac sticks. A father is told to kill his own child and says yes. God commands, "Thou shalt not kill," but he directs his disciple to do exactly that.

If one believes in God's might, and the direct intervention of God in one's life, wouldn't it follow that Abraham would comply with this directive? Abraham is proving his absolute allegiance to a single God, a concept that was radical at the time. When that God, all-powerful, issued a command, it stands to reason that Abraham would obey. If he did not, the consequences could be incomprehensibly worse than the loss of one life, even if that loss was his own child. On the other hand, it's possible that killing one's own child sits at the limit of the horror we are capable of comprehending as human beings. Perhaps a reasonable person trying to evade this fate would be willing to gamble on any other consequence.

As I listened to the sermon, it took me a moment before John, Angela, and the children flickered into mind, like a lightbox faltering as it switches on. According to John, something told him that killing the children was imperative, that he was engaged in a battle of good and evil, and he was on the side of good. He said that he had long seen himself as exceptional, chosen by God for some purpose, and had dreams where he battled demons. Where those thoughts and the message to kill his children came from is debatable, but

John said he believed at the time that it was divinely sent. Regardless of whether the culpable influence was psychosis or a spiritual force, there was no contradicting intervention at the final moment. No angel of God was present to stop John's actions. If any of us today were to kill his or her own child and attribute the imperative to do so to God, we would be labeled monsters of the most repulsive nature. The excuse of being commanded by God rings hollow, deceptive, or insane in a modern context.

I was stuck in my own thoughts on John and Angela when the rabbi's voice, rumbling with conviction, broke through.

"You say, 'I would not do that.' And you would be saying that you would not do what the source of all, the Creator of the world, God Almighty, told you to do," Rabbi Robert Levy said.

It can be difficult to conceptualize God's direct intervention in our lives, where "what God says, as we've learned, is what happens," as the woman at Good Neighbor told the group. We follow our own instincts, believing them to be our own. And we abide by the rules of society. These laws may be based on the codes of the Old Testament, forbidding us from killing or stealing, but if we break them, we will be punished concretely by a group of people who represent the modern rule of law.

Levy explained that, in the story of Abraham and Isaac, components of the Torah that usually work in union—righteousness and compassion—are separated from one another, acting independently. Abraham is the righteous one, behaving like a good disciple by doing as he is told. God eschews righteousness by issuing a despicable directive, one that seems seeded in the most jealous and manipulative impulse (prove to me how much you love me by sacrificing what is most precious to you), but then sweeps in at the final moment, offering compassion. Levy told the congregation that it is up to us to look for the points where righteousness and compassion intersect, and that we must find balance in our lives between what is merely right and what is compassionate; we must be neither the bighearted rube acting on pure emotion, nor the coldhearted realist who uses the rule book as his only guide.

When we dole out punishment to criminals, we usually begin with righteousness, as we apply the rule of law, and then, later, we might consider compassion. In capital cases, this plays out when defense attorneys present mitigating factors, reasons that the person on trial might be deserving of compassion and therefore be spared the harshest punishment—death—and instead serve life in prison. The guilt or innocence of the person is not addressed at this stage, but rather how much of our compassion he or she deserves.

The binding of Isaac has been interpreted for centuries as a story with a lesson that we're meant to learn, while the crime on East Tyler Street seems worthless as any sort of guide. Rather, it's what crops up in the wake of the crime that summons tricky questions. How do we, as bystanders, react to an atrocity? Here, Levy's sermon is germane. How do we become the best versions of ourselves when confronted with another person who exhibits the worst behavior within humanity? Letting righteousness or compassion guide us would be simple. We could let either impulse take us by the hand, leading us willingly toward uncomplicated forgiveness or vicious revenge. Putting the pair together simultaneously, while also weighing the rest of the ingredients of the event, is a vast and consuming task.

• • •

I walked to the building, a few blocks down East Tyler Street. It stood, menacing and comforting as ever, indifferent to my attentions. Here was Mount Moriah, the site of the slaughter. I walked a few doors down, toward the house where I'd met Miguel Angel. No car pulled up this time. No glamorous girl was walking toward the house, bringing her Austin dazzle to the neighborhood. A speckled Chihuahua walked out of the narrow crack in the gate of Miguel Angel's grandmother's house, but the lanky young man was nowhere to be found. The German shepherds in the neighbor's yard rose and gnashed their teeth. I crossed the street.

I'd written to John asking about his children's names. During the trial, testimony indicated that his youngest was named after a volunteer at Good Neighbor—Mary Jane—but I wanted to verify the origin. Julissa, he said, was a derivation of her biological father's name, Julian.

> Johnny was named after me, I changed his middle name though to Stephon after the carector alter ego of Steve Ercal named Stephon Arket, the cool guy. Because my son would be cool like his daddy! ☺

You might recognize that character from the 1990s sitcom *Family Matters*.

> Mary Jane was named ☹ after a name I liked the sound of when I was about 15 or 16 when I first started smoking marijuana. Mean-

ing Mary Jane. I know it was inappropriate to name her after a drug but the name had grown on me through the years and I like how it sounded. Mary Jane Rubio. I liked it.

In another letter, I asked John about his children's personalities. Mostly, he wrote about Julissa. It made sense—she was the oldest.

Julie was my baby girl, I would shower her with kisses and hugs which she loved and drove her crazy with joy. She was alot like me, very energetic almost bouncing off the walls like me when I was a child. She was very sweet, loving, caring and innoccent. If I was sad she would hug me and pat my shoulder and tell me there there but in Spanish whish was all she spock. She was so silly and made me laugh alot seeing her. Rarely she would fight with Johnny my baby boy over things. She would share everything with him and even her baby sister Mary Jane. She was not always like this though. When I first met Angela and Julie they had it bad. Angela was with this guy that beat her and cheated on her but there she stayed becaue he would always tell her taht noone else would ever want her. It took me alot of work to get that kind of thinking out of her head but she started reallizing she was of great value and not worthless like both of us had been told all our lives.

John saw himself as Angela's and Julissa's savior.

All the fighting and screaming would scare Julie and I honestly believe she was tramotized because even though she was 1 she did not speak a word nor was she potty trained yet. Girls develop faster than boys so she should have been talking by then but she was not.

Within 6 months of being with me she was talking non stop and even learned to use the potty. Angela would tell me she was too little for that but I told her she was not and I was right. One afternoon Angela and I were enjoying talking like we always did like good friends and out of nowhere Julie comes saying "look daddy, I did poo-poo." With the potty I had bouth her in her little hands. She really did go by herself and I was soooo proud of her, hugged her and told her she made me very happy. From then out she would just run to me and tell me "Daddy, daddy me pee-pee or poo-poo." I would take her bottoms off and she would go running like that to the restroom while I laugh from how cute she looked. Johnny was more of a tough guy, trying to boss everyone around even though he could not talk at 1 yet except some small stuff but I taught him to walk. He would pull on Angela, Julie or me if we tryed to get off the bed because he wanted us to be with him. He would get ontop of us to try to pin us down or rap his little legs around us. I would play with him a lot by pushing him down on the bed or lift him up and throw him gently on the bed, he loved that and would laugh like a maniac, jumping to try and get into my arms so I can throw him again. He liked to play ruff and sometimes Julie would complain to me Johnny was being mean. Then there is my Marie jane, sooo small, with the most angelic smile I had ever seen. She never cryed that I can remember because she was hungry, soiled herself or because she was sad. She was only 2 months but most kids that age cry alot. Johnny cryed but not alot alot. Mary Jane was somewhat darker skinned like my dad and looked to me a lot like my dad's mom whom didn't like me I may add.

In other words, things may have been hard, but in John's estimation his family had what mattered most, what he lacked growing up: two loving, attentive parents. In his telling, such love superseded stability, money, sobriety, or physical comfort.

I have always wanted to be a father since back when I was a little kid. I promised myself I would be a great dad, nothing like my dad and for the short time I did have with my kids I was, until this happened that is. I wanted someone to be a part of me, to give my love to and get love from. Many believe that Julie and Johnny were not my kids, maybe not by blood but they know no other father than me and I loved them better than any father would. You could ask anyone how I was with my children before this happened and they would tell you I was so loving with them. I never worried about responsibility problems because I have alwasy believed that love will always survive and if you love someone you will do what needs to be done to make the people you love happy. I will admit that I was not the best provider for my family. I had trouble keeping a job, always have. In part because I am slow, clumsy an dhave both dyslexia and ADHD. These are not excussess like many would think becaue if you read my school records all through out school that had been a problem I had to over come. I got better with time but never good enough.

Many of the routines of the family's life related to their community: the South Texas border. John rarely mentioned the border directly in his letters to me, but to picture the children one must factor in the ways they were shaped by their location. In Brownsville, it wasn't unusual that Julissa spoke only Spanish, even though she'd lived her entire life in the United States: her parents mainly spoke Spanish when together. Many children in Brownsville speak Spanish in their homes and neighborhoods and learn English once they arrive at kindergarten. Angela was from Mexico and had crossed the border illegally as a child, though this situation was also so common in the region that it was rarely mentioned when people spoke about the case.

Gloria Anzaldúa, the poet, called the border *una herida abierta*—an open wound. Bobby Byrd, the essayist, called it an alley between the home of a rich man and a poor man. The rich man needs the labor that the poor man and his family provide, but he also fears them and wants to control them.

The border inspires metaphor with its dissonance, displaying both concrete markings of its existence—a fence, a river, a Border Patrol truck—and an intangible impact on every facet of life in its proximity. The border puts the people on its edges in the constant practice of making comparisons. Depending on where you look, the alteration between one side and the other can be easy or impossible to perceive. Some differences are only a matter of degrees, such as the corruption that undercuts politics and business. But the differences can be arrestingly obvious, too, as when you cross the international bridge, striding from one country into the next, and encounter the smooth-faced teenager with a machine gun, his hand close to the trigger, or the group of Central American teenagers bounding across the highway and into the brush as they attempt to cross the river undetected.

Before I moved to Brownsville, I visited for a job interview at *The Brownsville Herald*. During that trip, a photographer from the paper took me to a friend's barbecue, where I met an environmental activist named Matt, who had moved to Brownsville from Minnesota after visiting with a college course that examined the environmental impact of the North American Free Trade Agreement. If I was taking a leap in moving to a border town for my first job, Matt was jumping blindfolded: with neither an official job nor independent wealth, he subsisted mainly off coffee and cigarettes that year, slowly losing muscle mass, and using his diminishing funds to pay for gas, rent in a seedy apartment, and cat food for two mangy strays he'd taken in. Matt invited me to come to Matamoros the next day with a reporter from the *San Antonio Express-News* who was writing a story about the garbage dump. I met him, the reporter, her photographer, and Domingo, a veteran environmentalist that Matt was informally learning from, near the international bridge. Together we drove across the river.

I had no sense of the size of Matamoros. I thought it would be a quick trip, but after we crossed the bridge we drove for more than twenty minutes through the dense city. The streets were clogged with cars and buses and pedestrians. People stood in the middle of intersections selling bags of nuts and potato chips and washing the windshields of cars with soapy water from plastic bottles. There were strip malls with grocery stores and movie theaters, love motels with cheesy neon signs, and horses grazing from strips of grass next to Pemex stations. There were houses made of found wood and sheet metal and mansions behind tall gates, and canals filled with garbage, and goats roasting on spits in storefront windows and hand-painted signs on buses, and schools with throngs of children in starched uniforms and people making long journeys home on foot along the edges of busy roads.

We drove out into a *colonia*, a neighborhood somewhere between a suburb and a slum. The roads transformed from potholed pavement to caliche to straight-up dirt. Ash from trash fires sparked the air. Finally we drove to the mountain of garbage. A rotten, burned brew of trash seeped into the car and our clothes. It smelled toxic. We saw the *pepenadores*, the trash pickers, who made their livelihoods collecting what they could from the piles. Children helped their parents pick through the hazardous junk for valuable metals or an unopened can of food or a pair of pants. We went to the neighborhood next to the garbage dump and met its residents. Everything in their homes—from the building materials to the food on the table—was scavenged from the dump. It was one of the most logical things I'd ever seen: an entire community living from a pile of discarded supplies.

That trip had a profound effect on my understanding of the border ever after. The sudden transition from one country to the next was astounding. No matter how poor Brownsville was in relation to the rest of the United States, I had seen the other comparison just across the bridge. The river snaked between the two countries, carving the curved edges of puzzle pieces. They interlocked, complicating each other, begging the answers to unspoken questions such as, how do we measure poverty? How does examining an alternative way of life help us to better understand ourselves, and what are the limits of that understanding? The trip made me want to stay, to begin discovering more of those questions.

Sometimes I'd talk to people in Brownsville who told me they hadn't crossed the bridge to Matamoros in decades. They'd be standing literally blocks from the river as they said this, but they regarded me with contempt: to them, visiting was a fool's errand, an outright request for trouble. I thought they were the ones missing out. A much bigger city, attracting world-class concerts, with more regal public spaces, more urgent and compelling stories for journalists, and access to many other points south, was sitting at their doorstep. Many people in Brownsville visited Matamoros more often than I did, even daily, and argued that the cities were really part of a single region that was falsely divided by a political line. But the division had recently become explicit. The rust-colored border fence had transformed the local aesthetic, and a pastoral landscape had become a broadly gated prison.

As the violence in the Mexican cities bordering the Rio Grande Valley began to increase sharply in 2010 when the Zetas Cartel split off from the previously dominant Gulf Cartel in the state of Tamaulipas, I started to feel the same fear of entering Mexico. The claims of oneness were quieted by gun battles. Bumper stickers reading NO BORDER WALL could still be seen around town, even though construction was under way.

Matamoros was one of a few places John had visited outside Brownsville. He may never have been on an airplane, but he had that basis of comparison to life in a foreign country, something many in the United States never experience firsthand. Angela grew up in

Matamoros and moved to Harlingen when she was about eleven years old. John and Angela loved their children, they had access to shelter and a soup kitchen, food stamps and medical treatment. As John has said many times since, they knew where they could go if they lost the apartment. They had more tools than some to support a little family, even though on the scale of US poverty, they were decidedly at the bottom. On this side of the border, they were sheltered from the extortion, lack of basic infrastructure, and institutional corruption that define life for many of the poor in Matamoros.

Maybe it would have taken years and medication and sobriety for John to become the father the children needed. I wanted to ask him questions about drugs and responsibility and the meaning of fatherhood, but it seemed cruel. These were the memories, whether they were truths or half-truths, keeping him alive in jail. He knew that he loved his family and that he was a good dad, at least compared to the standard that had been set by Angela's abusive former boyfriend or John's own father.

At trial, Dr. Brams testified that John had developed a superhero complex as a child, to try to control a world that was falling down around him. He was "a powerless little boy feeling powerful." John referenced this idea in one of his letters.

My family tell me I have a habit of sacrificing myself to please others, some friends have told me I have a superhero complx because I just have to help those I see in need.

CHAPTER 6

The Quiet Dead

Does my soul with its rich wealth of affections,
its unsatisfied yearnings for good, end all its strugglings in the
same grave where the body returns to death?
—HELEN CHAPMAN, 1851

It was a brisk day in Brownsville, unseasonably cool, and Professor Anthony Knopp and I were walking through the Old City Cemetery talking about the city's history. The cemetery, measuring a city block, is located on a small, sloping hill, close to downtown. It's protected by a brick wall, painted white, and the surrounding neighborhood is a labyrinth of one-way streets and alleys. The city's wealthy were historically buried here on the top of an incline. At the crest of the hill, gaudy mausoleums, intricate headstones, gated family plots, and towering statues called out the names of the dead. At the base lay the anonymous graves of those who couldn't pay for burial. Legend has it that when Hurricane Beulah tore through the city, these bodies were dredged up.

The low wall around the cemetery's perimeter presented little impediment to intruders, and many of the graves had been ransacked for jewelry. The plots maintained their eerie beauty, but there was sadness, too: The dead were defenseless. Anything could be taken from them, no matter how grand the burial. Their memories could be cherished or discarded depending on the fickle attentions of the living.

Knopp is Brownsville's local-history expert. He came here in his thirties, having studied Mexican history in college, and though he had since retired, he seemed to cling to his work in the manner of a smoker who allows himself a cigarette a day. Knopp was seventy-one when we took that walk around the cemetery, and wrinkles lightly imprinted his skin, like a delicate piece of paper that had been crumpled up and smoothed out again. His eyes were blue, but not bright. When he was excited about an idea and emotion was in his voice, those eyes sparkled and belied a more youthful man. He wore thin-framed glasses, muted sweaters, and favored jeans and sneakers when more professional attire was not required. He still taught one class at the local university, despite his frustration at the mostly uninterested students, and lived for the rare disciple who was truly intrigued by local history. Knopp knew how fertile the territory was for such a scholar. He came here from Minnesota, and Brownsville's historical intrigue (along with two marriages) had kept him anchored since.

For those who say Brownsville and Matamoros are artificially divided, a view from the air would confirm them as a single sprawling city, separated only by the jagged line of the river. But not much more than sparsely populated scrubland, farms, and palm forests were on the northern banks of the Rio Grande until Texas gave up its status as an independent republic and became the twenty-eighth US state in 1845. In retrospect, the annexation appears to be struggling President John Tyler's proudest achievement. Tyler, for whom the street where the murders took place was named, was referred to derisively as "his Accidency," having landed the presidency only after William Henry Harrison died of pneumonia (along with the cruel medical "treatments" of the time), after just thirty-two days in office. Tyler was not the ally that Harrison's Whig Party had hoped. His ascendancy to the presidency led to a public feud, complete with the nation's first impeachment attempt and threats of assassination. Aside from Tyler's achievement of annexing Texas, he is barely remembered and has become one of the most obscure presidents in US history. In Brownsville, Tyler is not so highly revered as to rate a street name; he is the recipient due to a grid pattern, whereby numbered streets intersect with those named for US presidents in the chronological order of their time in office, from George Washington—closest to Mexico—up to Zachary Taylor. The streets that intersect are numbered, so if you can remember the presidential order, your coordinates are easy to place.

Mexico had grudgingly agreed to accept Texas's independence on the condition it did not join the United States. After the annexation, the piece of riverbank that would become Brownsville was suddenly of strategic importance, as part of disputed territory, and General Zachary Taylor was sent here through scrubland with three thousand soldiers.

How had the city's power structure emerged and, with it, the divisions between the haves and have-nots—the Rubios among the latter group? Knopp told me that many of the wealthiest couples in the city have historically been unions between Anglo men who came to South Texas to find military victory or fortune, and the daughters of prominent Mexican families, many of them of direct Spanish descent, who had seen their country become part of the United States when Texas was annexed. To this day, there is a significant divide in Brownsville between the small upper-class contingent—many of whom descend from these early families—and new immigrants who have come to Brownsville to escape more extreme poverty in Mexico and stop in the valley before continuing north, sometimes staying permanently.

These legacies of inequality are tied to the architecture that remains. The jacales, where peasants lived, are no more, their materials too fragile to hold up. Now, wood homes, some just two or three rooms, sometimes built from improvised materials, dominate the area. The historical buildings that endure are the homes of wealthy and middle-class inhabitants, the places of business they built, and the military barracks.

Knopp took me to the site of Fort Texas, an earthen hexagon with nine-foot walls, erected in the absence of construction materials in 1846. Little is left of the original fort now, but you can still see the rise of the earth, a man-made addendum to the landscape. When Major Jacob Brown died in battle, it was renamed Fort Brown in his honor. Around 1848, the newly forming city was also named for the major, who provided centuries of unfortunate associations. *Brown*, as Knopp mused, invokes an aesthetic quality more commonly seen in the stretches of Texas border in the desert westward. Brownsville might be called Subtropicalville or Palm City were it named on the basis of looks.

Once the city was established, bricks were locally produced to build a proper barracks a half mile from those earthen walls. Over the next century, soldiers came to Fort Brown, bringing bits of the outside world with them. One such artifact was Helen Chapman, the wife of the first quartermaster at Fort Brown. Helen, a ninety-seven-pound New Englander, had a thin-lipped smile, pale skin, and straight brown hair that hung close to her cheeks. Her defining feature was a set of attentive dark-brown eyes, round and searching, serious but soft.

Knopp advised me to pick up Helen's letters, edited by her great-great-grandson. In a classic frontier narrative, Helen struck out from New York on the USS *Massachusetts* in January 1848, on her own apart from the company of a few other military wives, to join her husband in Matamoros. The sea voyage took seventeen days. In Helen's regular dispatches from the border, she told her mother both the simple details of her days—"they have delicious oranges here and I eat one every morning before breakfast"—and about politics, frontier life, and the plight of the Mexican poor.

Helen quickly adopted a bold attitude toward life in this unstable land. No summer was too hot, no disputed terrain too dangerous, no epidemic too dire. She came to thrive on this novel, renegade life.

"You must ask among yourselves why I am not afraid to go out in a country so insecure," Helen tells her mother. "I do not quite understand it myself, but I can tell you frankly and honestly that I do not know what fear is. I seem to have made up my mind that no soft indolent drawing room life is for me, that though exempt from actual labor, I must constantly be thrown into circumstances requiring activity, decisions and fearlessness."

Helen was troubled by the poverty she saw around her and worried about the welfare of the Mexican peasants. She experienced the epidemics that seized the frontier populations, such as cholera, and watched as nearly every family mourned a loss when the outbreak haunted the land, bearing its indiscriminate scythe. Her compulsion to describe the nuances of her day-to-day to her family back home made her the best chronicler of life on this stretch of the border during that transformative time, at least that we know of today.

Yet Helen's ideas would not have been regarded as consequential during her own time, due to her gender, which guaranteed her a subordinate station to the men who surrounded her. Though her views may have been influential among elected officials, and with future-president Taylor, Helen would not be the one remembered for their impact. Once she departed from the frontier, her legacy evaporated. There is no Helen Chapman Hall in Brownsville, and though the home where she lived in Fort Brown was recently reassembled, it was not done in tribute to her life, but because it could house an office and blend in with the other historic architecture on a college campus. General Taylor and Helen's devoted husband might have held her in high esteem, but definitions of noteworthy at that time did not include the wife.

It took 150 years for Helen's descendants to compile *The News from Brownsville*. Had her letters been lost, we would not know the history of the border as we do today. Helen's letters are a reminder of all the other narratives we are missing from this period—those native to the region, and those who did not have access to Helen's education. What remains is but a thimbleful of insight compared to what is lost.

As any cook will tell you, time is a powerful ingredient, altering profoundly the substance that it acts upon. What might become of the building on East Tyler Street if it was left undisturbed for reexamination in a century or more? Like Helen's writings, the building is not traditionally considered historic, or important, or educational today. But legacy cannot be realized without the passage of time, and the ability to synthesize the surrounding places and events into context. As I read Helen's letters, I thought of what might become of the building many years in the future. Maybe it could serve as an example of the atrocities that can occur when the system fails those in need, or what did or did not qualify as "insanity" in the legal system of this time, or what can become of a place when compassion is projected onto it instead of fear and hatred. But such a legacy would require the transformation of the way we currently evaluate modern events and would require our culture to prioritize time, and therefore hindsight, over more immediate concerns. Maybe it's not realistic to ask those of us living in the now to put a hypothetical future before our urgent necessities.

What would Helen think of the Brownsville of today, a place that men of wealth in her time predicted would rival New Orleans? She observed the divide of the muddy river, the Rio Grande, which separated Mexico's peasants from the northern wanderers who had been drawn here by a sense of possibility. Brownsville at that time was a potent, exciting land of opportunity, a flaming match that might be put to gasoline and combust, or simply burn out. The names of some of those businessmen—Stillman, Kenedy, King, McAllen—are still plastered around the Rio Grande Valley. Their descendants own land, businesses, and, to varying degrees, use that authority to drive public discourse and investment. Some of their names also populate the graveyard where Knopp and I walked together, though the remains of many wealthy citizens were eventually moved to the newer, more fashionable cemetery.

As for Fort Brown, it was never empty for long. Local landowner Juan Cortina's 1859 invasion of Brownsville caused troops to return to defend the city. During the Civil War, in 1863, Confederate soldiers set a fire in an attempt to prevent Union soldiers from seizing the fort. The fire quickly spread to Brownsville's downtown. The fort remained a contested site, due to its strategic importance for cotton shipping. Nearby Palmito Ranch was the site of the final battle of the Civil War, on May 13, 1865, more than a month after General Robert E. Lee's surrender.

Soldiers worked steadily to rebuild the fort, constructing dozens of new buildings. Many of these, which went beyond pure utility and had real beauty, are now part of the local community college. The old hospital is a pristine example of border architecture. Hand-fired bricks create a pleasing mosaic of peach, red, and sand, and covered porches with graceful arches encircle the building, providing protection from the sun. Now the fort is a jewel of the city, but during its heyday, it was an isolated, dangerous place. Soldiers died frequently after catching diseases from water taken from the Rio Grande. Food was hard to get, and soldiers dined on rotten bacon or flour that had been raided by mice. Helen, who did not imbibe, was shocked by the raging alcoholism of the soldiers, and fatal duels between armed men in the streets. Today, the fort is a carefully restored and often-visited center of education and local pride. Then, it was a stage for death.

Once the infrastructure of the fort was improved, its most peaceful era began. More illness, including a yellow fever epidemic, imperiled soldiers, but there were no battles.

Shortly after the turn of the century, a railroad was built through the city, connecting it to Mexico. The population swelled in response, and the use of irrigation helped the region's crops become more profitable.

In 1906, the city became a flashpoint in the national press when news spread of what would become known as the Brownsville Affair, the details of which remain disputed today. A battalion of African-American soldiers had been stationed at the fort, and on a sweltering mid-August night, gunshots were heard throughout the downtown, killing a bartender and a horse, and wounding a town constable. The white commanders of the Twenty-Fifth Regiment said that all soldiers were accounted for and were asleep in their bunks. But the townspeople produced used bullet cartridges that matched the soldiers' weaponry. All 167 infantrymen were dismissed by the army, despite the fact that none had been found guilty of wrongdoing.

In his 1970 book, *The Brownsville Raid*, John D. Weaver advanced the theory that the soldiers could have been framed by racist townspeople. By 1972 Nixon granted a pardon to all the soldiers. The story remains ambiguous, debated by historians. The truth may never be known, except to the dead.

In 1936, the Port of Brownsville opened, the second major business connection the city had established with the world. Two years later, Charro Days began, a festival celebrating the region's culture and its ties to Mexico, intended to boost tourism and draw prospective residents.

At the end of World War II, soldiers departed Fort Brown for the last time. Like so many of our national memories, which boastfully recollect victories in battle while lamenting the dead, Fort

Brown's legacy is a complex history of violence. When that violence is cloaked in love of country, the fort becomes an indispensable part of our collective past. While disease, alcoholism, and racism are mentioned in some accounts, they are mere footnotes. Instead, the fort is remembered for the glory of war, a symbol of Brownsville's eternal significance in shaping the modern boundaries of our nation. Today, the site of the fort can contain, with seeming ease, the gruesome acts of combat and the peaceful, meditative practice of teaching and learning. What was once a hospital has been transformed into the stately office of a university president. What was once a morgue where the bodies of yellow fever victims were dissected became an accountant's office.

It's hard for the building on East Tyler Street to compete. More than a decade after the tragedy, it felt more powerful, with its unpredictable bricks and slanted doorways, than the rise of earth where Fort Brown originated. But history is determined using the power of memory—a power measured in the resources and will of the living. We invest dollars and moments in one place over another. We identify the lessons that might be learned by a new generation, celebrate certain leaders and achievements, and damn others. And as we forget, we destroy. It is a silent violence. We cup our hands over the mouths of the dead, shutting our eyes and choosing to forget them without a conscious thought.

CHAPTER 7

A Corner in the Good Life

No one is going to want to live in those memories.
—FELIX SAUCEDA, NEIGHBOR

I walked around the chain-link fences near the corner of East Tyler and Eighth Street and stood on the sidewalks in front of people's yards. "Hello! *Hola! Disculpa!*" I'd call out, until someone emerged from a dark doorway, the lights dimmed inside the home to diminish the heat.

Around the corner, an orange tree spilled fruit onto the sidewalk and a man lounged inside a car with the passenger's door open in front of a little house with lattice fencing and a new coat of paint. The grass had been scraped away and a tidy dirt lot remained. From inside the front room of the house, the distinct excitement of a soccer announcer's voice blasted Spanish syllables into the street from a TV set.

"Hello? *Hola! Disculpa!*" I said from my post on the sidewalk.

A middle-aged man with a graying mullet came outside. He was wearing black cotton boxers and nothing else. I told him I was writing about the building around the corner.

"I used to live in that building," the man, named Sixto, said in Spanish. "It's uninhabitable."

"Did it bother you to live there, knowing what happened?"

"No, that didn't bother me. But I just couldn't live there. I was on the second floor and there's only one bathroom for all the apartments up there," he said. "The apartments don't have water, nothing."

Like Mr. Mendoza, one of the other neighbors, Sixto looked at the building pragmatically. No water, shared bathrooms—these concerns weighed far more heavily than the lives of strangers.

He seemed anxious to get back to the soccer game, so I tried some more houses. At one, a woman curtly told me the owner wasn't home and shut the door. At a yellow house that had been converted into a legal office, the young secretary said she was afraid to tell her boss, who was from Houston and didn't know the city's history, what had happened down the street. She didn't like working on the same street as the building and suspected that ghosts were haunting the block.

At the University of Texas at Brownsville, Carlos Gómez, an art professor, painted a portrait of John during his first trial. The local news had been on in his studio, and Gómez glanced at the TV set as John's eyes looked directly into the camera.

"It blew me away," Gómez said. In John's eyes, Gómez saw rage, evil. The image hit him, he said, like a brick.

He wanted to capture that evil in a painting. The result is a portrait in shades of fiery red and yellow, rendered with long brushstrokes. The piece, *John Allen Rubio Asesino*, was one in a series of five hundred paintings that Gómez called vignettes. He aimed to reach a thousand.

Children, Gómez said, are sacred in South Texas, and John's actions violated a fundamental belief that such things do not happen in a community so oriented around family. At the first opportunity, Gómez got rid of the painting, giving it to the permanent collection at Washington State University. Gómez thought the painting worked technically, but he didn't want the negative energy around him. Still, he felt it should be seen.

"We need to look at these things, because I think if we can recognize them, we can avoid them." Some atrocities, he said, come out of the void, striking at random. But not this case.

In 2010, after John's direct appeal resulted in a new trial, his attorneys argued for a change of venue, saying that the community's intimate knowledge and emotions about the case would preclude objectivity. In Barrio Buena Vida, it was hard to find anyone unfamiliar with what had happened, as it was whenever I mentioned the case to friends or acquaintances, or anyone I came across in Brownsville.

At the change-of-venue hearing, John's attorneys called witness after witness, trying to prove that all opinions here were biased. Father Ricardo Garcia, the pastor of Mary, Mother of the Church in Brownsville, had visited John in jail and described how easy it had been for him to see extensive information about John's case, including a confession video that was posted online, through a simple

Google search. Father Armand Mathew, a priest for sixty-one years in Brownsville, spoke of the hate the case had generated in the community, a reaction he found unacceptable.

Q. Is there anything about the nearness or the proximity of the apartment where it happened and the people who are involved that aggravate that, in your opinion?

A. Well, yes. I think the memory of the event is still very fresh in many people's minds. How could it not be? And so I think that that is bound to have an effect. I—you know, in my opinion, I don't think that anybody can be aware of this event and not have emotions that linger about it. And so I think even to this day—you know, I believe further, I don't care who we are, myself included, we cannot have that kind of emotional experience and set it completely aside. I don't care how sincere we might be, I just don't think that we can have an experience like that and not have it affect us directly always.

John's attorney Nat Perez Jr. told me that, in arguing for a change of venue, he was trying to protect his client from a bloodthirsty public. "People were saying they need to take him to the nearest mesquite tree and string him up," Perez recalled.

In the end, John was granted a change of venue to Hidalgo County for his second trial, in a courthouse about an hour from Brownsville. By then, Armando Villalobos had been elected district attorney, and he felt strongly that a death sentence must be secured to achieve a sense of finality. During the second trial, Angela took the witness stand, telling the events from her perspective, but John did not. Again, John's attorneys fought hard, and again he lost.

Across from the building, on East Tyler Street, I watched a man park and lumber out of his car. He limped toward his house, tilted his head, and drained the dregs of a Diet Coke.

Felix Sauceda, seventy-three, had lived on this street his entire life. He told me in Spanish that he was sure that no one would live in the building, even if it was fixed up.

"Do you believe in spirits, ghosts, things like that?" I asked.

"They say they're there. Personally, I haven't seen them, but they say yes."

According to Felix, two factors conspired to cause John and Angela to commit the murders: drugs, which make you "do things you will regret your whole life," and desperation.

"Not because of madness?"

"Yes, well, everything goes together. People, when they don't have something, they go crazy. It's like when you love a woman a lot and she leaves, you want to die alone or the opposite?"

But what if the city wanted to change the building and make it better, what would he think of that?

"They're not going to get anyone [to live there] because no one's going to want to remember what happened. That's what I think."

Many of the people I'd spoken to wanted the building gone, but when presented with the possibility that the city could make something better of it, they agreed, skeptically, that might be a positive step. Not Felix.

Felix told me about an incident at a clothing store downtown some years ago. The roof flooded and collapsed on the customers inside, and several people were crushed to death. These things happen, he said.

"For a time it stays in your mind, but then you forget it like everything. But at the beginning it makes a big impact. They were children—children! We think more about children because they're innocent, angels. We don't think so much about them [the parents]. Because they're the bad ones, we don't think so much about them."

Is there a grain of something, *un grano*, that we could learn from all of this?

Felix began to laugh.

Something that perhaps we could use to improve things after such a tragedy?

"No, no, no."

Why?

"Because he who takes drugs takes them alone, and these are the things that happen! If we told stories of everyone who is in prison, it's infinite. Nothing else like this has happened because things like this happen once in a lifetime, no more. Hopefully we're not going to see something like this again, because it's not pretty."

But a similar crime had occurred a few hours away in Laredo, just the week before I spoke with Felix. A man took his wife's two children to a hotel, and when the police came knocking on the door, he shot the kids and then himself. Felix told me such things happen when people are desperate. I asked him why desperation would lead people to kill, rather than to look for help.

"They looked, but they didn't give it to them."

94

"I think there always are other options."

"I know there are!" Felix said. "But when a difficult time comes and nobody helps you, no one listens to you, they leave you alone . . . I don't know how to explain it. . . . You go to your neighbor's house and ask if they could lend you three dollars to eat and they say they don't have it. You go to another [neighbor] and they don't have it, no one has it. You're frustrated and you have hungry children. And you kill them. That's how people think."

You cannot know the power of desperation, Felix was saying, until you experience it in its raw form. Desperation can fuel acts that would otherwise be incomprehensible. And if you've never been filled with that kind of quaking, hysterical desperation, you simply cannot fathom the way it can make you behave.

Felix told me about the woman who lived across the street. She shot herself with a rifle after being duped by a lover. Another neighbor who owned a store was killed with a machete.

Legends were piling up like a stack of bodies.

"I'm going to tell you something. Keep digging and you're going to learn more."

As I moved to turn off my tape recorder, I noticed a splotch of black ink on the plane of brown skin in the unbuttoned *V* of his shirt. Felix pulled down his collar so I could see. Jesus Christ presided over his chest.

CHAPTER 8

Angela

I don't know what happened to my mind.

—ANGELA CAMACHO

I looked for Angela's mother's home on the outskirts of Los Fresnos, Texas, ten miles from Brownsville. Los Fresnos, a sparsely populated ranching town, stretched from Brownsville toward the Gulf, alongside resacas and salt flats and the rodeo fairgrounds, with grapefruit groves and trailer parks, the land as unruly as its residents.

I had a possible address for Angela's mother from an online database and drove off a farm road and into a little neighborhood—two dozen houses on big lots along a road shaped like a figure eight. The neighborhood was a mixture of country and suburb. Some yards were filled with junked cars, others with chickens and turkeys. Idling slowly down the street, I searched in vain for the number. A man was trimming his hedges and I stopped to ask if he knew which house the woman lived in, referencing what had happened. Just ten miles away in Brownsville, everyone I met immediately understood what I meant by the Rubio murders. Here there was no such recognition. "I think I heard about that, a long time ago" was the closest I could get. I was further impeded by confusion over Angela's mother's name, of which I'd seen multiple versions. No, they didn't know her. They didn't know which house. In this way I continued, around the figure eight, looking for any house where someone was home.

Finally, I walked up to the stoop of a neat home on a smaller lot, and the family inside directed me to the correct one, just two doors down from theirs. The entrance to the porch of the small yellow house was blocked with a piece of plywood. I called out until a woman came to the front door. I told her whom I was looking for. This woman, large and intimidating but not unfriendly, recalled merely hearing something about the crimes.

"She's my mother-in-law," she said of Angela's mother. "But she's not here. She's away." I asked her if she knew about the crimes, and she, too, said she'd heard something about them, but didn't have much information. Her statements had a finality, and I left my name and number on a little note, explaining why I wanted to speak to Angela's mother. I got in my car feeling hopeful. Maybe I'd hear from her soon.

A couple of days later I went back. Maybe this time she'd be home. The woman came outside again, and again I told her that I was checking to see if her mother-in-law was home. No, she explained, she's not here. And she's not going to be back for a while. She's up north. I didn't understand what "up north" meant, exactly. Dallas? Canada? Everything was north except Mexico and the rest of Latin America. She said that her mother-in-law didn't have a phone, and they didn't have a phone or electricity at the little house. I wondered how she would contact me when she did get home and got the message.

I waited a week and tried again. This time the woman had a visitor and seemed less sympathetic to my mission, or maybe I was just interrupting some important business.

"I don't think she's coming back," the woman said.

I asked if she'd received this news since the last time we met.

"I just don't think she's coming back." I stood there for a minute more, hoping for some additional bit of information, but that was it.

I looked again at the house and the goat with icy-blue eyes standing in the neighbor's yard. The children lived here for a few months in 2002, after they were examined at the Brownsville Kiddie Health Center and found to show signs of medical neglect. Angela's mother took them in, until John and Angela completed parenting classes and drug testing.

Where does Angela belong in this story? She, too, is in prison for murder, serving three simultaneous life sentences that will leave her eligible for parole in 2045. I wrote to her several times requesting an interview but never got a response. At first I wondered if maybe she couldn't read, but when I called the prison, they told me that another inmate could easily read a letter to her, and I realized that she must be ignoring my request. I could only speculate: Was the subject too painful? Perhaps she didn't have anything more to say. Maybe she was just sick of being asked the same things over and over or was afraid that giving away new information could jeopardize her chances at parole. Maybe she was suspicious of the media, as she had every reason to be. When I found out that she had responded to a television reporter, Mireya Villarreal, and granted an interview, I wondered if my correspondence with John might be the reason— maybe she saw me as an ally to a man who had become her enemy.

Angela has a low IQ, tested at 62 as a fourteen-year-old. The threshold for mental retardation is 70 or below. In 2004, she tested at 51. According to criminal law, when a defendant is assessed for mental retardation, both aptitude and adaptive behavior are taken into consideration. Angela pled guilty and, in exchange, avoided a possible death sentence.

Her attorney, Ernesto Gamez, has a law office on Eighth Street, one block down from the building. You can see it from his parking lot. I was seated in a conference room with two taxidermied wild-cats, both wide-eyed as they identically caught a pheasant with an outstretched paw. Though not large in stature, Gamez was a brooding, intimidating presence. I asked him how he felt when he saw the building, which was incredibly close to his office.

"It has a stigma of an evil presence of what happened. It reminds me of the horror that took place, the carnage, of the kids." He spoke slowly, looking at some point in space with intensity.

Gamez said Angela was quiet.

"She was easily influenced. She was limited in conversational skills, and she was so docile and passive. And she felt that her kids were not being adequately provided for and that they would be in a better place somewhere else than what she could provide for them. At times she was psychotic and hallucinating of seeing a lady in black who was always around. A lady-shadow was always around."

Gamez spoke about darkness again and again as he talked about her case. He called the building a "historical remembrance of black death," said Angela's look had a "blackness," and, of course, spoke of the image of a lady in black.

I asked Gamez whether he thought Angela believed these hallucinations were real.

"I know there are dark forces, having experienced, not a near-death experience, but a death experience," Gamez said.

In May of 2008, five years after John and Angela were arrested, Gamez said he saw demons for the first time. "I didn't imagine it." Gamez had suffered a heart attack that left him legally dead for several minutes, and in a coma for six days after that. "There is no rational, logical medical explanation, other than the grace of coming back and giving me a second chance." To him, the demons are not a vague vision, but a specific memory.

"They were compelling to take me to hell. They were reaching out. They wanted me but they couldn't get me. The grace of God wouldn't let them get me, but let me know they're there."

Gamez believed he'd been enlightened to another dimension.

"There is an inner being, soul, within us and wants to live and wants everlasting life. And it fears the abomination of everlasting darkness. I really appreciate, when I crossed over, my ranches meant nothing, my property meant nothing. I'm left with nothing. Nothing was important. You speak, not with your mouth, but your mind. You have no physical form. And I can prove it because I was dead. And all that spirit of yours wants is to reach that light I couldn't reach."

His voice commanded the empty room, rough and croaking, pushing past my attempts to ask questions during the long pauses between phrases.

"So I cannot say that what she saw wasn't real," Gamez said. "I don't make that judgment anymore—if she's crazy or sick or mentally retarded—no. I know they're there, and they make people do very bad things. Evil things. Demons' purpose in life is for us—to compel us to do bad things. There is no love with these creatures."

Gamez now visits churches to speak with their congregations about his experience. He brings his cardiologist to support the scientific aspect of the story.

To Gamez, Angela was like a child—quiet and aloof. She showed little facial expression and didn't have a complex understanding of what was happening around her.

"Other than she'd done something wrong," he said. "And there was remorse, remorse, remorse."

Ultimately, he was glad Angela got a plea deal. She would serve three concurrent life sentences and be spared the death penalty. Prosecuting attorneys were aware she could be found incompetent to stand trial and that her Mexican nationality might prompt added attention to her case, since Mexico opposes the death penalty.

The closest I've come to meeting Angela was the hour or so I spent watching a video of her telling two detectives how her children died. The recording was made on her third day in custody. She wore an oversize blue shirt, and she was small and sweet looking, dwarfed by her thick, wavy hair. Her face was absent of guile or virtually any emotion. She'd been through the worst trauma imaginable, and the tape portrays a woman with nothing left inside. With the detectives she was calm and compliant and respectful, in a way that disturbed me: Had she simply been compliant during the murders? Was compliance the essence of her crime?

Angela told the detectives about coming to Harlingen from Matamoros as a child. She didn't detail what this meant exactly—swimming across the river or walking across the bridge and overstaying a visa. She went to Los Fresnos High School until she was a semester shy of graduation, then got pregnant with Julissa and dropped out.

She was living with her boyfriend, she told detectives, until he got arrested for burglary and went to prison for six months. Then she went to live with her mother and then her sister, moving back and forth. I went to Cactus Road in Los Fresnos, which Angela mentioned in her interview with detectives, and found a neighbor who remembered the family. He told me where to locate the plot where their house once stood—a grassy field directly next to the railroad tracks. The house had since burned down, he said, and only a pile of debris beside a stand of trees and the faded path of a dirt driveway remained. This was a parallel in John and Angela's lives: both lived in homes that eventually burned to the ground.

Angela knew her boyfriend, Julissa's father, was cheating on her, and she in turn cheated on him with John. When her boyfriend found out, Angela said he threatened her and her child, but before he could act, he was thrown in jail and she went to live with John.

Angela believed she was pregnant when she and John first got together, but only by about a month. She named her son John Stephan Rubio, and the couple lived with Julissa and the newborn in an apartment on Jackson Street, also in the downtown area. John had a job at McDonald's, and Hilda came to live with them. John said that they were given free rent in exchange for some work he did painting and fixing things around the apartment complex. Soon, Angela would tell detectives, things changed.

A. We stayed there for some months, and then we were on the street—on the street. Yes, on the street.

Q. What do you mean by "on the street"?

A. Because we didn't have any place to stay.

Q. Where did you stay exactly?

A. In parks.

Q. Here by downtown?

A. Wherever we would go, like corners—

Angela said that the children were placed with her mother around the time she became pregnant with Mary Jane, when Julissa was two years old and John Stephan was about four months old. John and Angela took parenting classes for several months to get the children back. By the time they did, they had an apartment in the building on Eighth and East Tyler, though not the same unit where they would commit the murders. John had been working at the Golden Corral, a buffet, and Hilda continued staying with them in their new apartment, though they tried to hide this from CPS. Lorena, a prostitute, also stayed with them for a couple of months, Angela said. She and John had become friends after partying together at the Hotel Economico.

Angela told the detectives that an employee from CPS visited two or three times a week, and admonished her for the dirty state of the apartment, but also brought free diapers. The CPS employees stopped monitoring them several months before the murders, once the family had completed all of the necessary requirements and John was working again at the Golden Corral.

The detectives were big men and asked the questions precisely and patiently, reviewing answers and saying them back to Angela to ensure their veracity. About halfway through the video, the detectives asked Angela to show them the placement of different events on a rudimentary map of the apartment, sketched in chalk on a blackboard. The camera zoomed in on the blackboard as Angela drew a stick figure of

John, showing the spot where Mary Jane's life ended. Throughout the interview, Angela adds the diminutive *ita* to the end of words, as in Julissa's *cabecita*, in place of *cabeza*. Her daughter's "little head." It's a term of endearment, jarring in the context of the conversation.

In the video, twenty-three-year-old Angela looks calm, much as Gamez described. She's detailing the gruesome deaths of her three children, but she explains the specifics with no agitation. She's so young, petite, and has a kind, cherubic face. In subsequent photographs and on the witness stand, the Angela who has spent time in prison is scowling, and her short frame carries extra weight.

Angela gave three different statements, on three consecutive days—the day the crime occurred, and the two days following. The first two were written, and the third was videotaped. In the first, she said fears of witchcraft accounted for her and John's actions. In the second, financial stress was to blame. In the third, which was videotaped, she fused these two statements, relating that both issues were at play. During the competency trial in 2010, Angela said that she gave the second statement, about financial strain, after a detective told her that was John's story. She seemed most intent on protecting John—matching his story if she thought it would help. When questioned in court, she said that she had lied to do so.

I'd asked Gamez whether he had a sense of Angela and John's relationship.

"In her own way she loved him, yes, and believed she was doing the right thing or involved in the right thing."

I asked Gamez if the tools that a court of law uses to treat such actions could be reconciled with the spiritual powers he now believes to hold such influence over people's actions.

"There seems unfortunately to be a disconnect in our law and the actuality of demonic presence that overtakes one's soul and mind. The law says if you do this, this is how you should pay." He knocked on the table. "But the disconnect is, the law doesn't balance out that this type of earthly demonic presence is capable of making, having people do evil things, that they wouldn't normally do, but for that demonic persuasion."

The rule of law was not sympathetic to the influence of religion, no matter how those enforcing the law might privately feel.

"They just say, 'You do it, you pay for it,'" Gamez said. "They say, 'You're responsible for your own actions.' However, the Bible is filled with lessons and parables of Jesus Christ casting out demons, and these people become whole and forgiven of their sins. The law doesn't have that forgiveness. It doesn't matter if you're possessed or have a presence of evil. You're responsible for it, period." Gamez saw this as a double triumph of the demons. They managed to both push the individual to commit the act and fool his fellow man into condemning him for that transgression.

"I really thought about having a defense that this was potentially a person who might have got involved in doing something that it wasn't the person doing it, it was the possession having them do it," Gamez said. "That makes them not responsible for the conduct, and they have this evil possession. Because what happened here was just horrific and not ordinary and not common."

Because of the disconnect he spoke about, such a defense couldn't realistically be pursued. Instead, he had his client choose between the possibility of the death penalty, and a plea bargain.

"These are high stakes: life or death. So, she chose life."

Mireya Villarreal, a correspondent for CBS, had once been a reporter for a Rio Grande Valley news station and interviewed Angela on camera in 2007. Due to the gag order during the trial, Angela hadn't yet told the community what had happened in her own words, outside of being questioned on the witness stand or shown speaking to detectives in video footage.

"Some people would say this type of thing scares them," Villarreal said. "I was always more intrigued than anything."

Villarreal wrote Angela a letter, and she wrote back. "It was kind of like exchanging letters with a child, with a kid. Everything from her handwriting to her grammar, the way she wrote sentences and described things, she didn't have the same level of communication as other adults."

Angela agreed to have Villarreal visit the prison and conduct the interview on camera. The letters were indicative of what Villarreal would find when she met Angela in person—a grown woman whose affect reminded her of a child.

When they met, Angela denied stabbing the children or helping John kill them. She said John convinced her that witchcraft had been performed upon them and that the kids were possessed.

"I start believing everything like a little girl," Angela told Villarreal. "I don't know why, but I start believing everything like a little girl."

Villarreal wasn't living in the valley when the crime happened and said she entered the situation judgment-free. She thought Angela had clearly been deeply in love with John at the time of the crime. It was the two of them against the world, outcasts even within their own small circle.

"She was very cognizant that the intoxication of being in love with him was part of what drove her to do it," Villarreal recalled.

Some were sympathetic to Angela's plight. In 2010, a letter to the editor of the *Herald* titled "Give Angela Camacho a Second Chance" read, "Poor Angela was one of the victims of John Allen Rubio and she gets punished. It seems to me that not enough justice has been given to her. If Angela is going to live in her own hell knowing that her children are gone and not coming back, is that not punishment enough?"

But most reactions to Villarreal's interview were vitriolic.

"They were so disgusted by her," she said, "and didn't think she deserved a platform to explain what happened."

As for Villarreal, she found the story made her a more sensitive reporter. Once she landed a gig in a larger market, San Antonio, she was quickly tasked with covering several more cases of mothers murdering their children. Three occurred in six months.

"I felt like I had a better idea of what these women were going through," she said. "It's easier not to rush to judgment and to be fair in these kinds of stories."

I went to Angela's mother's house again after several months. Two cars were parked out front this time, which seemed promising. One of them looked to be in good shape. Someone must be home.

As I approached I heard a jingle. A skinny cat with a tan coat and piercing blue eyes walked through a hole in the neighbor's fence. It wore a ribbon with a little bell around its neck, the kind that looked as if it had come off a Christmas tree. The cat approached me with caution.

A little green car, one I recognized from months ago when I'd come to the yellow house, sped down the road and then pulled into the yard. The driver, a middle-aged man, waved at me. *Buenos días,* I said when he got out of the car, and approached him with a note-pad. I told him whom I was looking for.

"*No vive aquí,*" he told me. She doesn't live here.

Did she move?

"*Sí, qué necesitas?*" Yes, what do you need?

I want to do an interview with her, I said, about her daughter Angela Camacho.

The man looked at me again, and I could see the traces of revulsion on his face. Reporters are always coming here from the TV channels, he said. She's not here. He waved his hand, the way I had to the cat a little while earlier, as if to say "scat."

I figured it was time to give up. I closed that line of inquiry in my mind. But I'd never spoken to Angela's mother, and the possibility was, however minute, that she would have been willing if she had the choice. After two years, I drove back again. The same man was there, and this time he told me that he was Angela's stepfather and explained at length why he didn't want to talk to me. I saw myself then through his eyes, as an emissary of sorrow. I asked if I could return again when Angela's mother was home and did so at a day and time he named. She walked into the front yard, listened to me for a minute, then dismissed me. She was courteous. I got into my car and drove around the figure eight, back onto the country roads, and back to Brownsville.

John with Mary Jane

Angela with John Stephan

*(Photos courtesy of
John Allen Rubio)*

CHAPTER 9

Don't Read This Chapter before Going to Bed

I would do anything for them.

—JOHN ALLEN RUBIO

In the beginning of March 2003, John and Angela saw friends, ate their meals at Good Neighbor, and took care of their children. John had lost his job busing tables at the Golden Corral in December, and Angela had given birth to Mary Jane in January. By March, Mary Jane was two months old, John Stephan was fourteen months, and Julissa three years old. Angela was twenty-three, and John was twenty-two.

The apartment was crowded with several other people who helped pay the rent. Hilda, often a roommate in other residences, was living in the rental, sometimes with a male companion. So was Lorena, a prostitute John had met at the Hotel Economico, whose legal name was Jose Manuel Hernandez. Lorena's boyfriend, Penguino, stayed over, too. Sometimes Lorena brought men to the apartment, and Penguino slept on the floor.

Without his position at the Golden Corral, John needed to find new ways to get his half of the rent together. He also, evidently, needed money to buy drugs: when tested during his probationary period for possession of marijuana, his urine was found positive for cocaine and marijuana in January and cocaine in February, and his probation officer filed to have his probation revoked. John did odd jobs, but that wasn't enough.

A. I had to sell my body. Not sell it, sell it. I mean, I would go to—downtown. My mom taught me this. She told me, "You want to make money, Son? I know an easy way for you to get money. You look good. You have a nice body. Men will pay for people like you, and they have and they all will."

Q. So you were basically a male prostitute downtown?

A. Yes.

John said he brought in about $80 a day and could usually make rent when he combined it with the money from other gigs. But John downplayed his sex work and told me it was not the norm.

He was also sexually involved with Jose Luis Moreno, whom he'd known as a young boy and met again as an adult. Angela seemed bothered by these extramarital activities, but John apparently didn't care. John wrote that Moreno gave him money, and that the relationship was "business and friendship only. He was the one who thought of us as a couple yet I never agreed to that." In court, Moreno called the relationship a "boyfriend, girlfriend thing," and said he never paid John to go out with him. Moreno was also seeing another man, Ivan.

John wrote to me that he tried to make the relationship clear to Moreno.

He was somewhat a friend but he wanted something more and that I could not give to him. I told him strat out from the first time I saw he wanted something more. He knew I could not nor would I love him or leave Angela for him. Angela did not like him or me doing that. She wanted for me not to go with him anymore. She said that she could find work as a baby sitter while I find a job. I didn't let her for fear that she too would be to independant and leave me as Gina did. Selfish I realize that now but back then I only wished to stay with her and my kids forever.

Moreno, a nurse, testified at the trial that he wanted John to leave Angela and live with him, and that he noticed John having what he called "absent seizures," or moments when John would stare blankly and unresponsively into space. Part of the prosecution's argument was built on the idea that, free of the burden of their children, John intended to run away from Angela and establish a new life elsewhere.

Two weeks before the murders, John and Julissa went to Bigo's, a Mexican restaurant, to celebrate Hilda's birthday. John put in an application to work at the restaurant. Afterward John and his brothers went out bowling. John was smiling and laughing, Manuel recalled. It should have made a good memory.

Hilda testified that, when the family got home from this outing, Angela told her she didn't want her living there anymore. Hilda went to stay with a friend nearby.

In the days immediately before the murders, Lorena was staying at the Hotel Economico with a client, a man who worked at a carnival that was in town. Penguino had stopped by the apartment smelling of spray paint, and John chastised him, Penguino would testify. It put a rift between the two men, and Penguino decided to leave. He didn't return.

John often huffed paint, but would tell a psychiatrist that he'd been on a binge for two weeks straight, and hadn't been eating or sleeping. While he claimed he stopped a few days before the murders, he could still feel the spray in his system. The drug had put a rift between John and Angela. She didn't approve of it, John told the psychiatrist.

Moreno's testimony portrayed John as frequently out of the house socializing, even though he had a new baby at home and two other small children. On the Friday before, John went to the carnival with Moreno and Ivan. They stayed out until three in the morning, then Moreno dropped John off at the apartment without going inside. The next day, Moreno came by to pick John up, but John told him he was busy taking care of the children. John's brother Rodrigo dropped his kids off and John watched them for a few hours. That night, John asked Rodrigo for money.

"I asked to see if he can try and get a job," Rodrigo remembered. "And if not, I would help him out then."

Rodrigo had helped John in the past and didn't always approve of his choices. Once he lent John $10, only to find that he'd spent it on Polaroid film to take pictures of the kids. Those would be among the only images of the children when they were alive.

"I thought it was kind of dumb," Rodrigo would say of the Polaroid purchase on the witness stand. "He needed something else at the house, like cleaning supplies or food." Ultimately, Rodrigo said the decision to buy the film to take pictures of the kids was "thoughtful" of John.

The question of money wasn't unusual.

"He was pretty much dependent on most of us."

That night, after 11:00 p.m., John left with Moreno and they watched a movie at Ivan's house. On Sunday, Moreno wanted to take John to the beach, but when he came by the house John told him to leave—Angela was angry with John, apparently for spending so much time with Moreno.

At trial, many of those testifying had trouble remembering precise timelines, so it's not always clear what happened when, or whose memory is the most accurate. During that week, a friend, Maria Elena Alvarez, also known as Beva, came by the apartment with another friend. It was Beva whom John and Angela had stayed with for a couple of months when Child Protective Services placed the kids in Los Fresnos. The kids had been sick days earlier, but Beva said medicine was in the apartment, which was dirty.

"Well, it was always dirty," she testified. "In other words, it didn't look like anything out of the ordinary."

John and Angela ate at Good Neighbor, where they also received their mail and got a notification that there was a problem with the paperwork for their food stamps.

Irma Longoria, an employee at Good Neighbor, saw John on Monday, March 10, the day before the murders, his eyes swollen. She'd never before seen him like that.

"Are you sick?" she asked.

"No," John said. "I haven't slept all night." He told Irma that he didn't have money to pay the rent, and that they were going to be thrown out of the apartment. But he didn't ask for help—instead, he walked out.

It was a beautiful day, sunny and in the seventies, with a breeze that usually came in from the Gulf that time of year. In the afternoon, John walked to the home of a man who knew one of his brothers, near Good Neighbor. John didn't know the couple, but he'd seen their car. He needed a ride, and it didn't hurt to ask.

The man's girlfriend, high school senior Melissa Nuñez, answered the door. John seemed to know that the car was hers, she testified, and asked for a ride to the Brownsville Medical Center—he was hoping to get Julissa's medical records and straighten out their problem with the food stamps. Melissa agreed to drive them. John sat in the passenger seat, despondent. He stared out the window in silence, making no effort at small talk. Angela was quiet, and the kids were asleep in the backseat.

"Thank you," John said when the ride was over. Angela said nothing.

The children hadn't been well, Angela would say in court. They'd been acting restless, crying through the night. It was different from the image John conveyed in his letter, of baby Mary Jane who hardly ever shed a tear.

It's hard to say when the story of the murders began, precisely. There are many potential beginnings—the childhoods of the parents, the first time John did drugs, or when the children returned from Angela's mother's house. But the afternoon of March 10, 2003, is the turning point. That date marks the confluence of those other stories with other beginnings, when the trajectories of their lives converged like sea winds fitting together into the twist of a hurricane.

John and Angela came home from the Brownsville Medical Center on a bus. In looking back, it's tempting to wonder how small changes in the day could have shifted things in another direction.

What might have happened if Angela had offered a thank-you to Melissa, and she'd stayed to drive them home, avoiding a bus ride during which John's paranoia seemed to amp up? Is it possible that they could have come home and gone to sleep, woken up in the morning, and walked, as a family, to Good Neighbor for breakfast? Or what if someone at the medical center had recognized that John was acting strangely? One hopes, looking back, for the events of the day to veer in another direction. Every moment feels like one in a series of mistakes.

On the bus ride back to downtown, another passenger offered a piece of candy to little John Stephan, and John told Angela it could be poison, an alarming logical leap. They got off in Market Square. There—surrounded by little restaurants; La Movida, the bar where Hilda worked; the Hotel Economico, where a Molotov cocktail would crash through a window and envelop the top floor in flames; and the tower of the Immaculate Conception Cathedral—John and Angela said they saw a woman with scratches on her forehead. They were less than a mile from the apartment. The woman, John claimed, had the mark of the beast.

"Run, run," Angela would recall John saying. "Don't allow her to look at your eyes."

They ran back to the apartment, a couple toting an infant and two little children, careening down the sidewalks of the city's one-way streets, past the used-clothing stores, the palm trees, the *hierberias*, the cats prowling in front yards. Also: the police cars, the county and federal courthouses, and the city jail.

When they returned home, Angela said they used the ritual of the *huevo* to "sweep" Julissa, passing the egg over her body and then cracking it open in a glass to check its yolk. They looked at how the egg floated. What did it tell them?

"That they did evil to her," Angela testified. Later, an expert on the use of the *huevo* would tell me this version of the ritual was inauthentic—eggs are usually used to heal rather than diagnose, and Angela and John would have needed a *curandera* to interpret the meaning of what they saw when the egg was cracked open.

Beva stopped by the house that night, and said John didn't permit her to see Angela. However, in her statement to detectives, Angela remembered seeing Beva and telling her that she was feeling strange. "I feel very bad," she said. "I feel as though something is happening to me." Beva had come by several times over the previous few days, so it's possible that Angela incorrectly recalled when this conversation took place.

Angela also told detectives that a friend had asked John to come with him to buy beer, so he could use John's ID. Later, when they looked for his wallet, which held their share of the rent, they couldn't find it. Police would locate the wallet, with more than $100 cash, under one of the beds.

Near midnight, Hilda came by the apartment after her shift at La Movida. She testified that she could earn more when she drank with her customers, so she would often lose track of the half glasses of beer she imbibed during a shift. Her friend gave her a ride to the apartment. She stood outside knocking for half an hour, but this didn't strike her as unusual because John and Angela often couldn't hear knocking if they were in their bedroom. Finally, her friend beeped the car horn and John answered the door. Hilda's intention, she said in court, was to give John $125 toward the rent the next day, when it was due. But she didn't tell John about this plan.

Angela was cuddling with the sleeping children when Hilda's arrival woke her up. "We were hugging each other, the girl on one side and the other girl in my arms." Hilda testified that John was mopping the floor in the third room of the apartment, and though it was near midnight, she didn't see anything strange about that. Instead she offered to help and rinsed the mop with Clorox. In her statement, Hilda said the children "looked okay." She changed into her nightgown and planned to go to bed at the apartment, despite Angela's insistence a couple of weeks earlier that she leave.

John asked Hilda about the rent. Rather than engage, Hilda stuffed a few items of clothing into a plastic grocery-store bag and prepared to go.

"Mom, why have you been doing witchcraft on me?" John asked Hilda calmly.

Hilda was surprised at the question. "I don't do it to my own enemies, much less my sons."

In Angela's version of the events, Hilda left the apartment at around 3:00 a.m., but John put the timing at around midnight. During that time, Angela felt increasingly tense.

When the family was alone, Angela said the children woke up and started crying. They seemed frightened and wailed for several hours. Angela thought about taking them to a doctor, but because of the notification they had received about other benefits, she worried they wouldn't be able to use Medicaid to pay for the visit.

This transition is difficult. From this point forward, the only accounts of what happened are from John and Angela. John's statement to the police is confused and agitated, and it's debatable whether an account from several months or seven years later would be any more accurate. He told detectives Hilda was acting suspiciously nice to him, but subsequently changed his story and claimed she was being mean. He said Lorena stopped by the apartment after Hilda left, then that she came by much earlier. Angela also modified her account after speaking with detectives. When she testified in 2010, seven years had passed and her relationship with John had soured. But all that considered, the basic account of the crimes is as follows:

At around 7:00 a.m., according to Angela, John killed the family's pet hamsters with a hammer and some chemicals. John said the rodents were acting possessed, fighting with one another. Killing them, he claimed, would help the children.

This detail about the hamsters is striking. It's an almost childlike act of aggression, existing in its own subgenre of violence. This was clearly not a case in which a person with a vendetta set about committing revenge. Instead, someone who had previously sought out these animals and fed them, played with them, maybe used them to entertain his children, had suddenly disposed of them with the unfeeling rancor of a Greek god. John told detectives he flushed the hamsters down the toilet. After that, he nailed the back door shut.

"My daughter started to talk like my grandmother who had passed away," John said in his statement. "Julissa started to laugh in an evil way and started making growling sounds at me. The other two babies started to do the same thing." In his confession, John described it this way:

A. And I said, *"Buela, quien?"* And I remembered what my grandmother used to do, little details, so I asked her, "Is it you, Grandma?" She said, "Yes." "What did you do with my daughter?" She goes, "She's right there," like she was inside my other girl, like Mary Jane. I said, "What do you mean? That's Mary Jane, that's not you." "No." I said to her, like, she was trying to give me—like tell me, but she couldn't say it, like, *"Yo es ella, y ella es yo."* [I am her, and she is me.]

Q. What she was trying to tell you, was that she was—

A. She was in her body—

Q. That your grandmother was in Julissa's body?

A. Yes.

Q: And Julissa's body was in—

A: In Mary Jane's body.

John said Julissa used scissors to cut the tape he had placed around an electrical socket to protect the children. He thought she was trying to give the scissors to John Stephan to cause him to electrocute himself.

In his written confession, John placed much of the blame on Angela for what happened next. Angela got the knives, he writes. Angela told John she'd rather kill the children than have them be evil. "I told her no, I did not want to kill them even though my grandmother took over her body."

In Angela's statement to the detectives, she said that John grabbed both Mary Jane and Julissa, then yelled for Angela to help him as he decapitated Mary Jane. She held on to the baby's legs. When they were finished, Julissa was crying. John grabbed her next, and Angela held her legs as he killed her on the floor. In testimony, Angela described it this way:

Q. And what was Julissa doing?

A. Screaming.

Q. Okay. Was she moving?

A. Yes, sir.

Q. How was she moving?

A. Her little feets.

Q. Okay. And what was John Allen Rubio doing?

A. He was trying to cut her head.

Q. While she was moving?

A. Yes, sir.

Q. And while she was crying?

A. Yes, sir.

Q. And what did you do?

A. I was crying and holding her.

Q. And what happened?

A. She died.

Q. Okay. How did she die?

A. With no head.

Q. Okay. So he cut her head off while you were holding her feet down?

A. Yes, sir.

Q. And what was your reaction to that?

A. I was crying. I couldn't think. I was just crying and crying, looking at them, and I didn't believe that they were my babies. And I was looking at them, and I couldn't believe it.

In John's version Julissa died first.

> My wife Angela told me to go ahead and kill the children. My wife
> then went and got two knifes from the kitchen. I then picked up
> Julissa and she was still talking like my grandmother and growl-
> ing at me. She was strong and I felt like she could manipulate my
> mind. I was trying to put spring water on her. She started to shake.
> Julissa started to yell at me, "You are killing me, you are killing me."
> I then placed her on the ground and my wife held her down. I then
> started to choke her because my wife told me that I rather her die
> then be evil. My wife then gave me a knife. My wife was holding
> Julissa with her face to the ground and I started to stab her in the
> back of the neck and in the chest. I stabbed her a couple of times.

In John's version of the events, he decapitated the children because
they seemed to rise and revive after being choked and stabbed.

> I thought I had killed her but then she got up and started to growl
> again was yelling for us to stop. She yelled, "Mom, please tell Dad
> to stop." I then grabbed her again and I cut her head off with a
> machette. The blood started to gush and she stopped moving.

John said Julissa's lips continued to move after her head was cut
off. "That scared me the most."

After Julissa died, John told detectives that Mary Jane was looking at him.

> I grabbed Mary Jane and I was chocking her really hard but she

would not die. It was very hard because she was my own blood. I kept trying to choke her but she would not die. I think I then stabbed her in the back of the head. Mary Jane kept moving like she was going to come back to life. I tried to cut her head off with the regular kitchen knife but it was not cutting threw. I was looking for the machette but I think the witches took the machette. I then ripped her head off with my hands it was very hard but I managed to pull her head from her body. My wife started to cry and was telling please not my daughter. I told her that we had to kill them because an evil presence was in them.

We then both started to cry.

John told Angela to start cleaning up the apartment. John carried the girls' bodies to the kitchen sink and poured water through their throats. The couple put the bodies in trash bags and continued cleaning up.

Q. And this is the dress of—
A. A little dress for my baby, Julissa.
Q. So you used Julissa's dress to clean up her blood?
A. Yes, sir.

They cleaned for a while, then took a shower. John told Angela they were probably going to go to jail, and that someone would inevitably find out what had happened. He'd tell detectives that he asked her if he could make love to her one more time, and she vacillated between no and yes, but in the end they had sex. During the second trial, Angela testified that she was forced into having sex with him.

Q. And what was the reason for having sex?

A. He told me that he was going to call his friends to rape me and he was going to kill himself.

In his statement, John first said they had sex before killing John Stephan, then corrected himself and said it was after. He believed the one-year-old was also possessed and needed to be killed. Angela said she fought John this time, but in her statement admitted that she also held John Stephan, or Johnny as she called him, as John killed him the same way he had the other two children. John told psychiatrist William Valverde that he saw John Stephan's head try to suck blood out of his severed neck. Thus John placed the head in a bucket of water.

At trial, Angela testified that she'd gone into another room and only when she returned did she see her son, decapitated.

Q. What did you do after you saw this?

A. I started crying again. And my mind—I don't know what happened to my mind but I start crying and asked him to kill me, too.

Q. You asked him to kill you, too?

A. Yes, sir.

Q. And did he try to kill you?

A. Yes, sir.

Q. How did he try to kill you?

A. Choke me, but he couldn't.

Neuroscientists tell us that we don't have a "memory bank," as we typically understand it—a place where memories are stored and retrieved when needed. Instead we reconstruct events as we try to re-create a memory. John and Angela's recollections differ, and we could attribute the discrepancies to many factors—lying, the effects of substance abuse, the passage of time. But in this story, the ending doesn't change. Whatever details might be altered, the children have died.

The couple cleaned John Stephan's body and then left the house and walked to Lopez supermarket, John's feet bare. They'd planned to buy milk that day, probably for the children. As though nothing had happened, they continued with their predetermined schedule. Angela was questioned about this trip at trial.

Q. Okay, and why did you go to Lopez?
A. I don't even know why, but we went and buy some milk and bring it back to the house and put it in the refrig.

A moment later, the attorney asked Angela about the walk to the store. Was she crying? Yes, she was scared. And how was John acting? He just seemed normal. They didn't speak. When they came home, John told Angela that a spirit was communicating with him, letting him know they would be in prison for a long time. Angela said nothing. All she could do was cry.

They placed the bodies of the children in black trash bags and a cardboard box.

That same day, Lorena made the ten-minute walk from the Hotel Economico over to the apartment for a change of clothes. John opened the door a little. On the witness stand, Lorena said John's lips were gold—an indication that he'd been using spray paint, though John's attorney was flustered by this at trial, saying that in

Lorena's original statement to police, she made no mention of paint on John's lips.

"My old lady tried to commit suicide last night," Lorena said John told her. "But now we're going to kill ourselves. Fuck everyone."

Lorena called to Angela, but said John shushed her, telling his wife, "Don't answer, don't let him [Lorena] convince you."

"You'll be sorry, John," Lorena recalled telling him. "You can't be acting crazy with those children inside."

Lorena said she threatened to call the police. After John shut the door, she claimed to hear the sound of a knife being sharpened in the apartment. Lorena returned to the Hotel Economico and never called police. She planned to return to the apartment, hoping John would calm down in the interim.

During the day, John and Angela washed the bodies of their children and cleaned up the apartment. Angela told detectives that John alternately talked about going to the cemetery to bury them, leaving the state, or simply waiting for the police to arrive.

Shortly before 7:00 p.m., Beva and Jose Luis, John's brother, stopped by. Beva testified that when John opened the door, he looked like he was "drugged up," and both he and Angela seemed serious. Normally, John would greet Jose Luis with a hug and a kiss, but he didn't reach out for either. John was holding a blown-up white bag, and it looked as if he'd been using it to regulate his breathing.

Jose Luis asked John where his mother was. John didn't respond. Jose Luis asked where the kids were. John said nothing.

Jose Luis walked back toward the bedroom and opened the door. He saw John Stephan's body on the bed.

Jose Luis grabbed the body. He realized it was a human child and put him back down.

"What happened? What happened?" Jose Luis asked John. "Where's the girls?"

Beva asked Jose Luis what he'd seen. He said he didn't know. Beva went to the bedroom to see for herself and returned crying.

Beva and Jose Luis left to get help. Initially, Beva said, Jose Luis didn't want to call the police, but John took his hand and told him, "I'll explain." Jose Luis stood there, frightened for a moment, before Beva grabbed his hand and they left the apartment.

As they walked back toward Beva's, they saw a patrol car in the street and flagged it down. Officer Efrain "Sonny" Cervantes was inside. He'd been sent to a domestic-disturbance call, but had mistakenly driven to East Brownsville instead of West. Realizing his error, he turned the car around and saw Beva and Jose Luis motioning to him.

Beva spoke through the window, telling him, *"El bebé no tiene una cabeza."* The baby has no head.

"It was like if I were to tell you, 'Come to my house, we captured an alien and I want you to see it. It's alive,'" Cervantes told me. He recalled that Jose Luis's eyes were wide-open, and both he and Beva were shaking their heads from side to side, looking as if they were in total shock.

Jose Luis and Beva climbed into the patrol car. On the drive over, the pair were talking in the backseat, though Cervantes said he could only hear through the thick glass something about heads. At about 7:00 p.m. Cervantes stopped the car at the building on East Tyler Street and the three got out. They approached the door to the apartment.

Inside, Angela was sitting on the bed, looking at the floor. Her hair was wet and partially obscured her face, but Cervantes recalled he could see her eyes through it. Angela wouldn't look up.

"What's going on?" Cervantes asked, cautiously entering the apartment. Behind him, Cervantes could hear the voice of one of the people who had flagged him down, talking to John.

"Tell him."

"The kids are in the back room," John said.

Cervantes walked slowly down the narrow hallway. The smell of bleach hit his nose. Through the open doorway to his right he saw a bare bed and an infant's crib beside it. All around were piles of clothes, some waist high. But the bed was sheetless.

Something was on the bed. Cervantes thought it was a headless doll, lying on its back with its arms up above its head, its knees drawn into its chest. Then he noticed the jagged marks around the neck. It was fourteen-month-old John Stephan Rubio. Cervantes touched the corpse to confirm that it was a human being, not the rag doll he'd optimistically seen at first.

"What happened here?" he would recall asking on the witness stand. He couldn't believe his eyes.

John, who had been seated, stood up and put his wrists together. "Arrest me."

Cervantes told everyone to exit what was now a crime scene. For years, the dirty clothes, deflated balloons, broken exercise bike, baby bottles, mattresses, shopping cart full of purses and debris, used condoms, and porn magazines would remain, waiting for jurors to walk through the evidence.

When backup arrived, John was transported to the police

station, about a quarter of a mile away. Officer Mike Cardiel patted him down outside the apartment, then put him in the center of the backseat of Cardiel's patrol car. On the short drive to the station, Cardiel testified, John calmly told him, "I cut my daughter's head. She was talking to me like she was possessed." After a silence, he added, "I remember seeing a bunch of cats outside of my window."

Q. So you took care of them, you fed them, you—how did you feel about the children? Did you love them?

A. Yeah. I adored my children.

Q. You loved them very much?

A. Of course. I would do anything for them.

John would also volunteer some thoughts about the murders in a letter.

The Bible says All things happen for good, though I still have trouble excepting that this had to happen for God to get my attention it sure worked. I've had to learn to forgive myself even though it still eats at me and it has been the hardest thing I have ever had to do. Just wanted you to know this so you can understand me a little. I have gone through a tramendence lose and tramatic event. No one seems to want to get to know how I feel about all of this. If you think about it, I mean really think about it and I really did believe I saw all that I saw and heard, the reality of having lost my children would and was a terrible hit to me once it sunk in.

John goes on to say that the motive presented by the prosecution—that he killed the children because he was overwhelmed by poverty—doesn't make sense. After all, they got their meals from Good Neighbor and knew where to find the city's free shelter—the Ozanam Center—though it's several miles from downtown. John says that the only "rational" reason for the murders was because "somethings crazy happened and I just snapped."

In another letter, John said he once poked his head into a bird's nest as a little boy.

i was looking at some beautiful bird eggs, white with some blue dots when something started attacking me from above. I looked and it was abird, not I am not going to say super man, a real bird like the eggs mama bird or the dad. i wasn't going to hurt them but she or he didn't know that so she/he was diffending its young. I tryed to swat it away and lost my grip.

John said he hit every branch as he fell down the tree.

CHAPTER 10

After

This type of thing happens once in a lifetime, no more.
Hopefully we'll never know something like this again,
because it's not pretty.

—FELIX SAUCEDA, NEIGHBOR

Macarena Hernández was the Rio Grande Valley bureau chief for the *San Antonio Express-News* at the time of the murders. She drove out to Brownsville from her office that evening and pulled up to the building late at night. News cameras, police, and dozens of neighbors loitered in front, hoping to learn some new tidbit. But for Hernández, those details—the ones that made other reporters' pulses race—plunged her deeper into distress.

"It just kept getting worse. And worse. And worse," she said. "Police always say in press conferences, 'This is one of the worst cases we've seen,' so I was used to hearing that. But this really was. Just the fact that the three little kids were all so young . . . It was just, like, how? What?"

After John and Angela were brought to jail, the street corner in front of the building quickly became a stage for votive candles, flowers, and stuffed animals. A cardboard sign was placed outside that proclaimed ESTAMOS CON USTEDES, ÁNGELITOS. We are with you, little angels. For a time, an image of the Virgen de Guadalupe graced the doorway. On the Thursday after the murders, a memorial was held on the basketball court of the Boys and Girls Club across the street, with about three hundred people in attendance. A neighbor, Nancy Garcia; sobbed as she told *The Brownsville Herald* that she'd never spoken to the family. "I feel so sad because I couldn't do anything. I wish I would have known."

Reporters came from all over the country to cover the story. Hernández's editors were eager to have her write regular follow-ups and attend the funeral. The mortician had carefully placed the heads back on the bodies of the children to allow for open caskets.

"It took many hours, but they were viewable," funeral director Lillian Kaye Guerra told the Associated Press at the time. "Everyone said they looked like little porcelain angels."

Julissa wore a white satin gown, Mary Jane a dress with flowers and a matching hat, and John Stephan a white suit and bow tie.

Before the service, Officer Cervantes, who'd been flagged down by Jose Luis, came by the funeral home. The murders were the first he'd dealt with in his career, and he was struggling. It had taken him two and a half hours and five attempts to write a police report less than two pages long. Cervantes didn't get home until five thirty the next morning because, he said, the police department was triple-checking every detail, to ensure that a technical error wouldn't get in the way of the criminals' prosecution. As the week progressed, he decided he needed closure.

"They opened the funeral home for me so I could go in and see these kids with their heads on," he told me. "I wanted to see them complete." The children, he said, looked beautiful. Peaceful. He carried that image with him from then on and, in the decade that followed, rarely spoke of the crime outside the courtroom, even to his wife.

Looking back, Cervantes could clearly see how the case had altered his life. At work, he'd proven his professionalism, and colleagues told him he'd learned more in a single day than he might have in years on the job. From then on, he approached every call skeptically, cognizant that a superficially routine visit to a Brownsville home could morph into something unimaginable.

It also affected his personal life. Cervantes had been young when his wife got pregnant, and he spent the next seven years working at a grocery store before putting himself through the police academy and becoming a cop. During those years of early fatherhood, he was focused on work and equated parenting with providing for his family rather than being present. But after he discovered the crime scene, his priorities shifted. When he went home the next morning, he walked past the shelf with his kids' storybooks and toys and kissed each of his daughters, one sleeping beneath a Hello Kitty comforter, the other under a SpongeBob blanket. As he looked at his five-year-old, he thought of Julissa. In the months and years that followed, he spent more time with them, fitting in an extra hour at home when he could.

The weekend after the children died, pallbearers carried the white caskets into the Guerra Funeral Home and laid them alongside one another. The aisles were filled with toys.

Elsa Guerrero, a seventy-six-year-old employee of the Lopez supermarket, told Hernández she had a soft spot for Julissa.

"What a beautiful family. I know I'm older, but if they'd given me the three-year-old I would have tried my best."

Angela's mother wept uncontrollably while Hilda silently cried. Later, they both released doves for the children, as did Julissa's aunt. After the funeral, it began to rain, and a woman told Hernández, "Heaven is crying." Angela and John were both on suicide watch in their respective jail cells, being checked every fifteen minutes.

Hernández grew up in the border town of La Joya, and as she reported on the murders, she was frustrated. "I hated that the only time we wrote about these towns along the border was when these really horrible things happen. This isn't really the narrative of the border. When it happened, I knew: we're going to spend a lot of energy on this story. In journalism we try and be objective, but we're also not objective when we only cover these types of stories and leave everything else out."

Journalism has its shorthand. "Run and gun" reporting refers to speed: get to the scene immediately and photograph or report as much as possible. Parachute journalists drop in from out of town, having prepared for a day or two before hitting the ground. They get the story and leave before public interest ebbs or they rack up too large of a tab for the publication. At a local outlet, a story like this might become a reporter's beat, meaning he or she would have first dibs on any news generated and would be assigned to watch it like a hawk.

But once that burst of attention subsides, most crime stories become footnotes. As Hernández suggested, to the world beyond South Texas, a city such as Brownsville is just an imaginary place, a spot on the map that's psychically blank until it's filled with bits of information that appear in national publications or broadcasts or films. These snippets are often limited to local crimes, and their perpetrators begin to populate that blank space, leaving out all of the regular people who make up the majority of the community. While the story may have been resolved from a news perspective, for the people who witness and survive such an event, its trauma has a long life.

Even for a place that's off the collective radar, something good occasionally makes its way into the mix—a championship sports team, the rescue of an endangered plant or animal, a talented artist, the local cuisine. But too much of what people learn about a border city, or small, poor cities generally, relates to spectacularly terrible events covered with shallow impatience. A camera shutter snaps, a neighbor comments on his or her shock. Those reactions remain preserved as the sole—and therefore final—word on what happened. The subtler details fade away, and the community, that network of friends and neighbors and strangers that reach out and help one another in the face of such a loss, isn't represented.

In her book *A Paradise Built in Hell: The Extraordinary Communities that Arise in Disaster*, Rebecca Solnit describes the way people band together in the face of tragedy, defaulting to our best, most charitable instincts as if we'd been switched back to a factory setting. "The possibility of paradise hovers on the cusp of coming into being, so much so that it takes powerful forces to keep such a paradise at bay. If paradise now arises in hell, it's because in the suspension of the usual order and the failure of most systems, we are free to live and act another way."

Solnit's book is concerned with large-scale disasters such as the earthquake that leveled San Francisco in 1906 and the destruction of the World Trade Center, which reconfigured entire cities and tossed their inhabitants into chaos. A heinous crime does not create that kind of absolute disorder, or, therefore, the reordering of the world in its wake. But such events do create confusion and need and inspire others to respond. Some of that reaction is vitriolic, but much of it is giving. Those bits of kindness doled out in the face of horror are often obscured by fascination with gore or left out of thirty-second sound bites that become the archive. While some generosity may be instantaneous, some takes time. The changes that spring through a community, both broadly and in the lives of individuals such as Officer Cervantes, go unacknowledged.

It took seven weeks before Dr. William Valverde, a psychiatrist, met with John. He said John showed the symptoms of paranoid schizophrenia, a condition he believed may have been exacerbated by the use of spray paint. Notably, the symptoms of schizophrenia typically begin to manifest in early adulthood. At twenty-two, John would have fit the mold. Many of those suffering from the chronic illness experience delusions, believe they're being persecuted, hear voices, and think they're on a special mission. Most are not actively psychotic the majority of the time; rather, the severity of their symptoms can heighten or subside.

John's timeline of the events, as he described them to Dr. Valverde, seemed radically off. He told the psychiatrist that he and his family were inside the apartment for seventy-two hours—a full three days—rather than approximately twenty-four hours that other testimony indicated.

But if John did have schizophrenia and was seeing and hearing things that weren't real, why did Angela blame her actions on the same illusions? Dr. Valverde attributed this to *folie à deux*, or a "folly of two," a French term for the rare phenomenon in which two people living in proximity sometimes share the same delusion. "There is a dominant individual," Dr. Valverde testified. "It is their delusion first, and then you have the other person who tends to be somewhat passive and becomes convinced that the delusion is correct and then supports the dominant person in sharing the delusion, or maintaining it in place."

Angela's characteristics matched some of those psychiatrists say can be found in the second party—she was mentally challenged, female, and had what some described as a passive personality. John wrote to me that, when he and Angela first got together, he tried to instill in her a sense of agency and convince her they were equals, "but she was so scared, she would just follow what anyone would say. She is sweat, loving, but gulable as well." Still, Angela's behavior wasn't as thoroughly scrutinized as John's, as she accepted a plea bargain and never went through an extensive trial of her own, and so her part in such a group delusion is not clear.

At the end of his first trial, after John was found guilty, one of his attorneys, Alfredo Padilla, told jurors that he and his cocounsel had intended to present evidence that might have inspired the jurors to have mercy on John, but John had instructed them not to do so.

MR. PADILLA: Mr. Rubio, it is my understanding, sir, in our discussions previous to this date, and on yesterday afternoon, it is your request that this jury assess death to you, sir?

DEFENDANT RUBIO: Yes, sir.

MR. PADILLA: And it is your belief that God has forgiven you for what you have done, sir?

DEFENDANT RUBIO: Yes, sir.

MR. PADILLA: And that you want to be with your children in heaven; is that correct?

DEFENDANT RUBIO: Yes, sir.

MR. PADILLA: That's all we have, Your Honor.

CHAPTER 11

Good Guys and Bad Guys

That story could have happened to me.
—EDUARDO RODRIGUEZ, FORMER NEIGHBOR OF ANGELA

Ed Stapleton worked in a sleek office near the strip malls and housing developments that edge Brownsville's north side, but he lived in a historic house in the heart of the city's downtown. Like the other attorneys and witnesses in the case, Stapleton was subject to a gag order during the trial, so he was adept at deflecting reporters trying to tack down a comment. After weeks of failed attempts to get him on the phone, I planned a stakeout when one of his friends gave me his cross streets.

The house looked as if it were plucked from New Orleans or Savannah and plopped down among the banana trees on Saint Charles Street, less than a half mile from Mexico. While maybe not the biggest or the grandest home on the street, for my money it would be the loveliest to live in. Knopp led tours of this block to showcase some of the city's most successful restoration projects.

Like the ragged houses a mile away on East Tyler, Stapleton's place was guarded by a big dog that waited behind a front-yard fence. I couldn't get past him to knock on the door, so I waited. A few minutes turned into a quarter hour, then a half. The late afternoon was bleeding into evening. Then Stapleton appeared, walking slightly laboriously toward his front gate, his hair gray, his face soft and tired, his body large and unapologetic. He looked like an attorney from a Southern classic—too big for Atticus Finch, but with that same calm and serious air.

Stapleton opened the gate and led me into a spare, formal living room perfect for uninvited guests. I told him what I was working on, and he agreed to speak with me later.

Stapleton's insights were sharp—distilled from the many months he'd spent contemplating the case and explaining it to the jury. But when he spoke, he was calm and matter-of-fact, never seeking approval or persuasion. He'd simply answer the question at hand, lay out his thoughts, and there they were.

Stapleton's reflections related in part to the propensity of some attorneys, law enforcement agents, and, indeed, people, to place convicted criminals into a category of society they deem dispensable. To him, killers act in a moment of inevitability—when the worst possible circumstances collide with a person primed for an act of wild transgression. John fit perfectly into this mold—poverty, abuse, and mental illness had continuously collapsed on him since the moment he was born.

"I certainly do not believe universally that there's any real volition that goes into acts like that. People do what they do because of forces that make them do it, and they have no choice in the matter," Stapleton said. "I know that my view of that is not the most common view, but I think it's supported by more life experience, and also I think it's supported by the science.

"The main difference between people in jail and those not in jail is not even innocence, in my mind. There's some correlation with poverty and your ability to buy your way out of problems. It doesn't have anything to do with being good or bad or moral or immoral."

It doesn't have anything to do with being good or bad or moral or immoral. That sentence hung in the air like a bubble waiting to be popped. It's an almost ridiculous idea—that those in jail are as good as the rest of us. Stapleton's conviction was stirring. I wanted to believe that he was right. I wanted to believe that he was wrong.

Stapleton was religious, and that was the reason he agreed to work on a death-penalty case. The force of his convictions came partly from the sermons he heard in church during his childhood, and partly from a formative event in his family: his father was tried for homicide after he killed someone in a drunk-driving accident. He defended himself in court, and was acquitted.

Preordination was at the heart of Stapleton's understanding of this fundamentally unjust world. Preordination, as Stapleton put it, posits that we are all destined to commit the acts and make the decisions that form the content of our lives, and that free will is a delicious illusion that allows us to struggle with morality and try to serve God. Stapleton, unlike many people, believed this even when he stepped outside the doors of his place of worship. When John and Angela were in the apartment that night killing their babies, Stapleton believed they were playing a part in the scripted drama that is humanity.

This view raises so many questions: Am I a helpless participant in my own life, waiting for the moment when something good or bad happens, laboring under the misguided belief that I'm choosing to type this sentence? And if everything is preordained, why not create a world full of beauty and happiness, devoid of pain and suffering? Do we learn nothing from our actions if we are already destined to do the next thing and the next without alteration?

In some respects, preordination is profoundly disturbing: Why try? What will be will be. But it also provides a cause for compassion in even the bleakest situation. John had no choice, it reasons. He acted as he was destined to. And who are we to judge a divine plan in action?

Every time I went to Brownsville, I had to visit the building on East Tyler Street. Was it research or compulsion? What would realistically change from two days ago? Those weeks when I'd gone without seeing the building, I would come back and find it the same. But it felt changed. Or maybe I'd changed. The weather got hotter and the air around the building felt heavier and full of poison.

I looked for patterns in the interviews and noticed a figure mentioned repeatedly: the devil. Was he involved? In John's letters he said an evil force was responsible for what happened inside the apartment. When I asked the neighbors if they were religious, I heard ambivalence in their voices, the moment they asked themselves, should I say this aloud or should I be silent? Maybe the devil had played a role in the crimes, the leading role. Maybe the devil had possessed the children, or, more convincingly, possessed John.

I put it to Stapleton. What about this belief—some may call it superstition and others religious faith—that John was possessed by an evil force? How did that enter into the trial? I expected him to dismiss the question and move on. Instead, he spoke with his usual calm, serious tone:

"That was an alternate theory—that he was, in fact, possessed by the devil, and we had members of the defense team that believed that, and I had supportive witnesses that believe that. I don't believe in devils or devil possession, but that doesn't mean that we weren't willing to advance the theory. We considered it. Legally it's not a defense. Possession by devils is not a legal defense. It doesn't acquit you. If you're possessed, you don't have the mental state. I think Mr. Rubio believes and believed he was possessed by devils. I think a lot of well-educated people believe the same thing."

Much of what Stapleton said conflicted, predictably, with what District Attorney Armando Villalobos told me. Villalobos, a tall man whose dark mane of hair was perpetually slicked back, had a salesman's smile. To him, John's case was the sad result of poverty coupled with drugs and desperation. According to the prosecution, John wanted to leave Angela and the kids behind and start a new life. The pressure of the responsibility was weighing hard. The family couldn't pay the rent and the notification they had received about their food stamps added to the stress. John was unemployed and had a new baby. He wanted to escape. So, he killed them, playing the part of the madman in hopes that if he couldn't flee, he would be found not guilty by reason of insanity.

Villalobos told me he didn't agree with glorifying the crime, or even remembering it. I asked him why not remember if something could be learned from it. Villalobos seemed skeptical.

"I mean, if anybody can learn from it, I'm all for that," he hedged, "but you're talking about a situation where the lifestyle of both par-

145

ents was something of their own choice. They decided to get into drugs. She [Angela] decided to stay with John although John was basically prostituting himself homosexually and had a relationship with somebody else. To me it was like, there are stressors that everyone has. It's just how you put yourself in those situations. These people put themselves in this situation." This view was meant to be tough but fair: people are accountable for their problems, and John made a series of bad choices.

Villalobos took office just two years after the murders. He was not the DA when John's initial trial took place, and once an appellate court granted John a new trial, Villalobos knew he was responsible for leading his office to a victorious and final verdict in the case.

"In the city and community there was a sense of wanting to get this over with," he said. "The longer it dragged on, the more it kept these wounds open."

Of course Villalobos would scoff at the idea that the devil played a role in the crime. And preordination? No, he held people responsible for their actions. To Stapleton, Rubio was a victim of his own madness, a history mapped out for him before birth. To Villalobos, there was simply no forgiving the unforgivable, especially for a person who did not lead an upstanding lifestyle.

"We as human beings want things to make sense," Villalobos said. "We expect things to make sense. Most of us follow the rules and have good reason when we choose to not follow a rule. But when you deal with criminals like we do, you learn that there's a percentage of the population that just does whatever they want with no regard for the rules, no regard for what makes sense."

He sounded cynical, like a hard-boiled cop, worn-out from too many tough cases.

Stapleton believed that the things we do are inevitabilities before they occur, that imprisonment or freedom are circumstantial, and that no essential difference divides us. To Villalobos, we are a civilized society with a small renegade population of bad eggs. There's no point in explaining away their actions—justice is exacted through punishment, not empathy.

The law sides with Villalobos: "In our system of justice, in order to not be held responsible for your actions, it's a very high burden. I'm glad it's a very high burden. You think these people are crazy because you say, 'Who would do that? Who would crash into a McDonald's and open fire? Who would leave their kids in a car and let them die in the heat?' Everyone has different opinions of what is crazy. Legally, the question is quite simply, do they know right from wrong? No matter how crazy they are, no matter how absurd, if they knew what they were doing was wrong, they're guilty."

The prosecution needed to prove that John didn't have a "severe mental disease or defect" that prevented him from understanding his actions were wrong. A lot of testimony was heard, for example, about John and Angela's cleaning up the mess after the deaths, as it points to an effort to hide the evidence. Their discussion about sex and the possibility it could be the last time, and John's alleged statement to Cervantes, "Arrest me," provided additional evidence that John and Angela were well aware of the nature of their actions, at least after the fact.

Angela would also testify that John had once mentioned the idea of killing the children, several months before it took place. She shrugged off the comment at the time, believing it was just silly talk, the way you might ask your friend, "What would you do if I died?" One of the most damning moments of the second trial occurred when John's lover, Jose Luis Moreno, testified that John asked him, about two weeks prior to the killings, whether Moreno knew how to commit the perfect murder: "He said that you could get away with it by saying that you were insane." Moreno also claimed that John wanted to take two of the children with him to Austin, to get away from Angela and Hilda and Hilda's boyfriend.

These signposts indicated that John knew what he'd done was criminal. But did that mean he did not meet the legal definition of insanity at the time of the murders? Dr. William Valverde, the psychiatrist who first evaluated him, said that while John may have understood society would punish him for what he'd done, it doesn't mean he appreciated the "wrongness" of the act itself.

"Much like a child, the impulse, the desire, that needs to be met, whatever it is this that pops into your head, overwhelms any sense of morality," Dr. Valverde testified.

The long-term effect of John's drug use was also debated at trial. It clouded the ability to discern between symptoms caused by brain damage and those caused by schizophrenia. Dr. Valverde argued the drugs would not cause hallucinations several days after they'd been used (John said it had been three days since the last time he did spray before the murders), but they could contribute to long-term delusions. His argument that there's a distinction between knowing an action has consequences and knowing that such consequences mean it's wrong was not persuasive to the jury. When reading about what John did, the visceral reaction may be that only a person out of his or her mind could take a kitchen knife to not one but three children's throats and force it through their flesh, their muscle, and their spines. Legally, however, that's not enough to grant a defendant a not-guilty verdict.

The prosecuting attorneys also built their case on the series of economic misfortunes that were piling up on the family, suffocating them and allegedly causing them to decide that the children would be better off dead. They had received a concerning notice about their food stamps, Hilda waffled with her part of the rent, which was due the day of the murders, and they had a third baby in an already-full apartment. Still, I've always found this notion—that poverty was the culprit—perplexing. If John wanted a fresh start, he could easily have left Angela and the kids. He had also made adjustments to hold on to them before, participating in parenting classes and drug testing to get the kids back. The couple had contacts with many agencies, including their daily visits to Good Neighbor, and John had even mentioned a plan to go to the Ozanam Center, a homeless shelter, in his statement to police. They'd faced desperate poverty before, and survived. There's no reason why blood would have had to be shed.

When I spoke to Stapleton and Villalobos, I got swept up in their conflicting perceptions of the moral dimensions that undergird the workings of a courtroom. Then I took a step back: Attorneys are paid to persuade. Best not to take their views too much to heart. Villalobos's paradigm, a clear division between the criminal and law-abiding segments of society, makes us all feel safer when another of the "bad guys" gets locked up. After all, they're bad guys. By his logic that's what they'll always be.

Then, in May of 2012, just a few months after our conversation,

Villalobos was indicted by a grand jury in a widespread corruption case and accused of accepting more than $100,000 in bribes and kickbacks. In one case, his greed helped orchestrate a plan that allowed convicted murderer Amit Livingston to go on the lam. He wasn't caught for seven years, until he was found in India.

When I talked to Stapleton after the indictment, I recalled Villalobos's statement to me. That only certain kinds of people commit crimes. That we can't expect to understand such people because they live outside the rules that govern society.

"His view may be changing now," Stapleton said generously.

Do you think that people who commit crimes tend to be quicker to condemn others?

"We call it the magic mirror. You hate things about people if you see yourself in them. I think people who feel guilty tend to be more judgmental." This concept had been part of Stapleton's closing argument at trial.

After Villalobos was found guilty, I attended one of his hearings in federal court. He looked calm. His eyes were down, that thick crop of dark hair neatly brushed and gelled. He wasn't frantically flipping through documents or nudging cocounsel to offer an explanation or legal argument. He seemed to understand what awaited him, one way or another: prison.

When Villalobos appeared for his sentencing, that air of tranquility was gone. His voice broke as he cried in the front of the courtroom, pleading with US district judge Andrew Hanen for a lesser sentence. His children, Villalabos said, wouldn't have him as a father during a crucial period of their lives.

"I'm not the monster they paint me to be," he said. In a letter the previous year, John told me he was "not the monster I have been made out to be."

Hanen spoke deliberately. He was aware of the responsibility that came with his position—a counterpoint to the lack of respect that Villalobos had for the public trust as DA. Hanen eventually sentenced Villalobos to thirteen years in federal prison.

Is it easier to believe that John is a "bad guy," and that what he did was "evil," or is it easier to blame the circumstances of his life? It's cognitively overwhelming to combine these factors, to see him both as the catalyst and the entity upon which other catalyzing forces acted.

Psychiatrist Michael Welner, hired by the prosecution, testified during the second trial. He had provided his expertise in a number of other high-profile cases, evaluating Brian David Mitchell, who kidnapped and repeatedly raped Elizabeth Smart, and Pedro Hernandez when he was on trial for the murder of six-year-old Etan Patz. By the time he took the stand, Dr. Welner said he had already spent about 275 hours on the case, at a rate of $400 per hour—a cost of $110,000. It was an extraordinary amount according to other forensic psychiatrists I interviewed. Welner founded the Forensic Panel, a group of experts to create oversight in the field, and developed the Depravity Standard, to compare the relative heinousness of crimes based on various factors. The standard aims to create consensus on terms that are generally held to be abstract and subjective—such as "evil." It's a quixotic pursuit that takes for granted that evil is a knowable quantity in our world, capable of comparison. Then again, so, too, is the conceit that a jury, presented with the evidence of a single crime, can understand it relative to a range of cases they have not considered. Dr. Welner believes the standard would ultimately make the court system fairer: when a large sampling of Americans can decide on such a metric, the regional and personal prejudices of individual judges and juries would be set aside, and juries would have a system to make their grave decision. Still, the underlying assumption that "evil" is capable of measurement seemed flawed, and counter to the scientific basis of modern psychiatry.

I asked Stapleton whether he thought Rubio or what occurred in the apartment that night could be termed evil. The question seemed absurd as it left my lips. The word could define the case, but only if you used a particular lens to view the world as a whole. Was Rubio evil? Was what happened evil? Is anything?

Stapleton said he didn't approve of the way the word "evil" is typically used—to exclude people from society and vilify them. They are damaged people, he said, not evil. "I don't buy into the idea that there's good people and bad people and there's a line that separates us out. I think we've got a little of every element in us, and if we don't recognize it, it's because we haven't looked at ourselves closely enough."

It took me a while before I decided to write to Villalobos in prison. I reminded him of our previous interview, then quickly got to the point.

You told me, when we spoke, that criminals are of a different segment of society, and that it's no use trying to understand their rationale, because they don't think the way the rest of us do. I can't help but wonder if your views have changed or evolved on this issue.

As with my first attempt to contact John, I posted the letter without a sense of expectation. After all, it might not be advisable to write to a reporter when you're still trying to get your conviction overturned. But, a month later, a response appeared in my mailbox.

Villalobos recalled being under intense pressure to pursue the death penalty in Rubio's case. His office conducted polling, he wrote, and concluded that the city wanted to see John sentenced to death.

> All these factors, plus the unsettling, shocking and unescapable images of the babies that were murdered, led me to conclude that at the very least, a jury should decide his fate.

He went on to say that different people handle prison in different ways. For some, solitary confinement is damaging, he wrote, but others adapt. Then Villalobos came to his final offering of the letter, an "observation," which came closer to a response to my question than anything that had preceded it.

> Once I was sentenced and led away to a holding cell, then off to the federal detention center, where I was held in isolation "for my protection," it was difficult not to think of all the people who had turned on me. People I had helped prosper, helped their families, helped their friends, and others in which we shared life changing events with. People I considered close friends. As you can imagine, it shakes a person's resolve and can cause a person to question friendship and trust. It puts you in a position that can definitely change your persona from a personable, friendly, easy going person to a bitter, angry individual, lost in the world. As I sat there in the dark contemplating those feelings, something very

unexpected occurred. The other inmates who were in isolation as well—they were not in there for their own protection, but rather for the protection of others. They were guys who were usually imposing, with ink images of various gangs and affiliations all over their bodies and faces. Guys who were hardened by their rough lifestyles and chosen path in life. Definitely the exact opposite of whom you would expect to find any kernel of compassion. But, these men, despite my years of prosecuting them, their friends, and relatives, reached out to me in those dark moments and gave me encouragement, gave me advice, gave me food, and most of all—gave me hope—that not all was lost.

I put down the letter. This was his answer—evasive though it might be—to the question I'd posed. His intended message seemed to be that criminals were indeed not as he had believed them to be, and that they were capable of greater compassion than some of his own close friends, people whom he saw as disloyal. But by couching his answer in this observation, he revealed that his original prejudices persisted: he still separated himself from the criminals—these inked and hardened men, who had "chosen" their "path in life"—as if Villalobos himself had not also made the choices that had led him to his cell.

I thought of Stapleton's belief that we are composed of a mixture of qualities, good and bad. That being convicted of a crime does not fundamentally make a person any worse than someone who has never spent a night in jail. Temptation would lead me to judge Villalobos, to lick my chops and relish the deliciousness of his conviction. The challenge would be to set aside that impulse.

I was blunt in my next letter: "I wonder, do you still believe that criminals are fundamentally different than other people, now that you have been convicted of several crimes?" He wrote back that he had to resign himself to being "referred to as a criminal." He defined a true criminal as "a person who has no regard for anything other than themselves and is constantly looking for ways to improve their life at someone else's expense and someone who has absolutely no remorse of conscious (all in the realm of committing a crime, harm or illegal acts on another)." He also wanted to clarify that his family had been rallying around him and added, "I have had a long history of seeing the good in people (almost to a fault) and most definitely have been compassionate—especially during my time as D.A." He said that this compassion was a source of aggravation for federal law enforcement officials who saw his approach as too soft. If this was true, the dichotomy between him and Stapleton grew cloudier, as every assumption seemed to upon further inspection.

That was our last correspondence. One passage stuck with me above everything else he wrote. In the ending to his first letter, he summed up the hope that the other men behind bars had given him:

Now granted, I don't see myself at family pic-nics with most of the guys I have met on this journey, it left me with a feeling that all will be all right in due time—like the image of new growth after a raging forest fire.

CHAPTER 12

Agua Bendita (Holy Water)

Get some holy water tonight.
—MINERVA PEREZ

I don't know how many times I went back to the building. I wanted to burn it into my mind, to own the memory, before it was destroyed or changed into something unrecognizable. I had the sensation that I knew it only partially.

The façade looked orderly enough from the street. The doorways varied slightly, and the paint seemed to change color inch by inch, but the structure appeared to be something understandable: an old two-story apartment building. On closer inspection, the neverending details undermined this simple definition. On the front, stenciled lettering was just faint enough to be unintelligible. The sloping sidewalks were another mystery: Were they once indented so cars could drive up to the gasoline pump? They upended my feet, sending me off-balance and close to stepping on the nearby broken glass. Every time I visited, I'd check in on the silent battle of street gangs whose graffiti was periodically whitewashed, wondering who was leaving their mark.

I visited on a sticky day and walked around with a notepad, taking stock of what new things I saw. I'd never noticed the banana tree growing in the neighbor's yard. The image smacked of fecundity—an abundant crop of small, uniform bananas practically dripping toward the alley. I wondered if a patient person was nearby, the custodian of this particular tree, waiting until they ripened.

Something unexpected occurred that day: A truck parked on the grass and a kind-faced city worker walked toward me. He asked if I wanted to check out the building, and together we traversed the grassy lot. In the past, I'd stayed on the sidewalk and in the alley, never treading in the tall, unkempt grass.

As we walked toward the back side of the building, I noticed a tiny, cartoonish cactus growing at a tilt. A dead papaya tree, perhaps killed by the previous year's freeze, was disintegrating on the far side of the property. Its pale carcass was as porous and intricate as coral.

Suddenly, an extension curved out of the back, like an unknown limb. I'd noticed this one-story house that shared a wall with the building on East Tyler Street, but I'd always assumed they would stand side by side in back, the small house dwarfed by its big brother. But instead of going proportionally back, the little house narrowed into a series of small, linear rooms. In this way it resembled an arm—conjoined to the building at the pit in front, but then moving back skinny and independent into the lot behind. An alcove formed between the appendage of the little house and the body of the building, and everywhere along the border were doors; doors to the little rooms of the house, doors into the conjoined armpit between them, and then doors from all the first-floor apartments of the building opening out into the peninsula of grass. There, the white porcelain of a forlorn toilet lay on its side, and a square of carpet marked the entrance to one of the first-floor apartments.

The city workers explained that they were closing off the building, but first they had to go inside to make sure they didn't shut in any squatters. One man had already started sealing up some rooms.

With the doors flung open and the insistent squeal of the drill boring unnaturally through metal, the building seemed like a surgical patient: it lay helplessly as it was unhinged and put back together, with a mix of new and borrowed parts.

The city worker said I could look inside if I wanted to, and I walked in through an open doorway to my right. It didn't take me long to realize where I was. Though the shape and size resembled a hallway, the lumps of clothes on the floor, dirty and shapeless as if they'd been through a flood, told the story. I'd seen it in pictures, though the mess looked fresher nine years ago when it was documented as evidence. I was standing in the crime scene. The doorway I'd stepped through was the same one nailed shut by John.

It was too dark. I couldn't be sure where my feet were taking me. All the court testimony made sense: the apartment was shaped like a hallway, witnesses had said. The rooms ran from one end of the building to the other with a door on either end. I could see the cracks of sunshine leaching through the doorframe, but not enough light came from any direction for me to know precisely what I was looking at. I feared I'd step on something in advanced decay.

Here was the heart of dread. It was not fearsome. It was fetid, noxious, hopeless. A deep and exhausting misery, a crevasse so bottomless that, in the blackness, all one could make out were the contours of despair.

I took photographs, using the flash to illuminate the room. But the bursts were momentary. I saw only glimpses:

The concrete floor. The kitchen sink filled with plastic bags, dirty bowls. The ladle hanging from a nail, waiting to be used again. A container of lard on the counter, a box of oatmeal. An upended mattress pressed against the wall. Red and purple artificial flowers forever vibrant in a plastic vase.

The contents of the apartment were preserved. Perhaps there had been squatters, vandals, addicts. But because the family had cobbled together the items they could find to make a home, it was hard to tell what was new and what was old. Later I learned that the brown stains on some of the items were dried blood.

When I got outside, I felt like running. The wet air was clean and I gulped it in, realizing I'd been trying to hold my breath, trying not to inhale the smells of the apartment.

They're going to seal up the door, I thought. They're going to close it up with their tools and I never have to go back inside again.

The city worker invited me to look inside the attached house. Not much was left there. Dirt caked the floors, and the long body of a garden hose was coiled like a snake. Light filtered through the windows in the small rooms, and brilliant green leaves could be seen between the metal bars on the windows. The light and the leaves evoked the peace of one of my favorite paintings, *Shadow Decoration*. The 1887 oil on canvas work by Charles Courtney Curran shows a woman in a simple brown dress and apron hanging laundry from a line. Through the white sheets the viewer can see the dark shadows of exotic leaves, revealed as verdant green in the corner of the painting. She sees the laundry, the pins, and the line, but she's surrounded by the friendly shadow-ghosts of leaves, representing an unseen paradise. In that portrait exists the possibility that you could be going through the mundane actions of your life—doing laundry or the dishes, say—but living in a different landscape.

Inside the apartment the possibility of escape shrank down in the darkness. I had looked at the building from the outside so many times. I'd watched and cataloged it, contemplated its codes and scars and memories. But the essence lay inside, sealed up beyond the doors of people's homes, where families' lives are privately kept. There lay the love that John and Angela showed the children when they were alive, the laughter. There, too, was the hunger and the drugs and the blood.

I called Brad, the photographer, and he came by to take some pictures before they shuttered the apartment. As soon as he was finished, I thanked the city worker and walked down the block to Minerva Perez's house. Minerva had lived in the neighborhood all of her sixty-nine years, always in the same house, two doors down from the building.

That day she was inside with her cousin, who had also grown up here. Minerva was warm, her eyes always focused on yours, with a face that invited you to smile whenever she did. She may have been the first advocate of the building's demolition; the children's deaths had never stopped haunting her. The children had been a fixture in the neighborhood, and she'd seen them daily when they passed by her house on the way to their meals at Good Neighbor. But years had passed since the city had started to discuss the demolition of the building, and Minerva was still in its shadow. It could be there for the rest of her life.

I asked Minerva what the neighborhood was like when she was growing up.

"You better believe it—it was real nice here. We didn't have cement. We used to walk. The blocks were dirt. Remember? And we had good neighbors. Los Chapas."

"All of those houses were neighbors," her cousin cut in. "The Benevidez, *aquí* [here]. Now, no *hay nadie* [there's no one]. Everybody's dead."

I asked them what they meant by "better."

"Now, *horita*, you cannot trust anybody, mama!" said the cousin. "It was a beautiful neighborhood, we grew up here! *No había gangas.*"

"There weren't gangs," Minerva reiterated.

They remembered that the building used to be a gasoline station, something I'd learned from the fire insurance maps from the thirties. Later, they said, it was called the Imperial. After that it was derisively called El Hotel de los Chiflados, the Hotel of the Stooges, for the elderly people who lived inside. The nickname might have come from a 1939 Mexican comedy. Minerva and her cousin told me that men used to drive up in taxis around the corner and whistle to the prostitutes on the second floor just a few years before the murders.

Minerva and her cousin talked about the old neighborhood with reverence: the families, the neighbors, the nuns at the Catholic school, the dirt roads. In Minerva's memory, all of it was better than what was there now.

"All the houses were beautiful houses," the cousin said. "But now there's *puro ratones*, there's rats and everything." The cousin, skeptical of me, told Minerva, *"Es muy grande la history para ella."* The history is very big for her.

The cousin said she used to live at the Imperial. She remembered the wives of shrimpers who lived there at the time. "They used to help us. The ladies, they were clean people, clean ladies! But ever since they killed these little kiddos there—did you get the story about the kiddos?"

I had.

I asked Minerva and her cousin when the building started to change, transforming from the nice place they lovingly remembered to the one they derided, that they wanted destroyed.

"When people moved, it started changing because people from across started to live there," Minerva said, referring to Mexico. "It's been more than thirty years."

"Thirty-five years," the cousin chimed in.

"They let it go, they let it go down," Minerva said. "But still people live there. They don't pay rent, they just go in there. Smoke pot and everything."

"Right," I said.

"I've been after the mayor so he can destroy it, do something, but they say they don't have the money. And now the city, the city, now they're saying the city bought it and it's the city's property. You can see I'm not lying, you can see lights at night in those windows, all those windows that are broken, I can see light. Me and Mr. Mendoza, we were outside and we can hear voices from inside."

"*Como* [like], right here, the Garzas were here," the cousin said. "They had the kids, the sons, they grow up here. We all grow up here. It's nice. *Ahorita*, now *vive una* Mexican lady she rented, she's not supposed to have ladies from Mexico hiding in there or whatever. It's not the same, mama."

"What I mean, it's not the same," Minerva started. "Sometimes I sit down outside and I figure out all the things that were my mom's friends, my neighbors here . . ." She closed her eyes, imagining.

"You close your eyes and you think about how it used to be?" I asked.

She nodded. "It used to be real nice, you know. But when everything happened . . . I'm not saying this whole neighborhood . . . just this side here."

Minerva said that the vacant lot next door had, at one time, been the site of a beautiful house. The woman who lived there had killed herself. Felix Sauceda had also mentioned this death.

"What happened to the house?" I asked.

"They destroyed it."

"Who did?"

"The owners," she said. "Because it was so old and they didn't want to fix it up and they destroyed it," Minerva said. "After ten, fifteen years."

"You have a lot of stories here, in this neighborhood," the cousin said. "I'm telling you the truth. You have a lot of stories. Then right over there in the corner, his name was Tony Rodriguez. Tony. *La pichona*." The pigeon.

"They killed him right there, too."

"They killed him over there with a machete. He used to have a store."

Minerva and her cousin recounted some of this story and some of that about the neighborhood. In their voices I could hear the pangs of nostalgia for a childhood that no longer existed. Even pleasant memories were tinged with violence, with suicides and murders and prostitution. Though Minerva and her cousin spoke a combination of Spanish and English, they both talked of the threat of people from "across," moving in and destroying the neighborhood.

"I wish you could go inside there and take pictures with some-body, mama," said the cousin.

"Well, I just did actually."

"You went by yourself?!" the cousin yelled, even louder than her normal loudspeaker pitch.

"You went inside?" Minerva asked, shaken.

"Into the apartment where they killed the kids," I said.

"You went inside? Mama, don't go in there," Minerva said. "It's bad. I'm gonna tell you why: there's some evil spirits in there. Better go to a church and get holy water because I'm gonna tell you why. The guy in the back, they went over there to that place at four o'clock in the morning, they saw a lot of things and they came out screaming."

Minerva looked at me warily, almost as if she were afraid to touch me again, lest she contract whatever I was now carrying. I listened to her admonitions, but I still hadn't processed all I'd seen inside the apartment. Something powerful resided there. Was it a bad spirit, as Minerva said? Is a spirit the same as a memory so visceral it makes a terrestrial home, nesting between the walls of its setting?

"The thing is, they should tear it down! That's what I want, but there's no one who will help me." Minerva was frustrated. The other neighbors weren't doing enough to rally to get the building demolished: the venom they had once felt had diminished, and she alone held on to it with the same intensity of years ago.

Too many people had died at 805 East Tyler Street, and Minerva worried that in its current condition, there would only be more death to come. Some vandals could start a fire. Her house could also go up in flames.

"Go to the church and get the holy water," Minerva urged. "*Se metió allí. Está malo*," she said to her cousin—she got in there. It's bad.

At the end of the afternoon, Minerva's voice got quieter and formality wilted away. She was too upset to play the hostess anymore and spoke to me like a confidante.

"You think this neighborhood has something?" she said.

We could hear her cousin on the phone with her daughter, telling her that a reporter had gone into the building where the kids were killed.

"She's going to tell the whole neighborhood," I said to Minerva, and a laugh came out of her, full and vibrant, like a sigh of relief.

When I left Minerva's house, I thought for a moment about going to the Immaculate Conception Cathedral, five or six blocks away. Minerva was sure the holy water would provide an antidote to my actions. I nearly went, if only to be respectful of her wishes. Instead I drove home and took a shower.

In the district clerk's office I sorted through a box filled with folders and papers and unearthed a stack of photographs, eight-by-ten, glossy color images that had been printed with an abundance of ink. I paged through them one by one. Here was John, young with a week's worth of facial hair, a plaid shirt with a dark collar, standing against a wood background. He was looking just beyond the camera. He appeared to be around twenty-two, his age when arrested, but it didn't quite look like a mug shot, too informal. Another picture showed a happy Julissa. I recognized the image from the newspaper archive—she was smiling so widely that it almost looked as if she were baring her teeth. But unlike the picture I'd seen at the *Herald*, this photo wasn't cropped. She was sitting on a bare, dirty mattress and seemed to be holding an empty videocassette box, though I couldn't make out the title. In front of her, in the corner of the photo, was a little boy, his face turned away from the camera. John Stephan was in a third photo.

He was sitting in a yellow-and-blue plastic swing, the kind with a secure bar for little children, suspended by ropes. He wore only a diaper. He was pale and his eyes were angled down toward the ground.

The next set of images seemed to rise up suddenly, like an external force, though I was showing them to myself with the flipping motion of my hand. A child's face was on an appendage divorced from its body. Little bodies of children, headless, were covered in puncture wounds from knives. And then, close-ups, in glossy ink that felt almost thick on the paper, of the wounds where heads were torn from bodies. On those wounds, the blood washed away, were flaps of skin I'd never seen on a human body, never imagined. Thinking of them now as I type this makes me tremble. I raced through the stack of photos, trying to see as many as I could as quickly as I could, until I felt that I might black out or throw up or fall to the carpet in tears.

The first time I was told about the murder case, when I came across the documents in the filing cabinet near my desk, the cops reporter told me he'd seen the crime-scene photos. Something in the way he said it indicated a superior level of knowledge. I could read the file all I wanted, he subliminally told me, but until I saw the photos, there was something I just wouldn't understand. Since I'd been researching the case, I'd rationalized many times why I did not, in fact, need to see the photos. The same information could be found in the coroner's report. Maybe I was in denial. I wanted to understand the case, but some part of me was holding back, afraid of what might happen if those images were imprinted on my mind.

Once I saw the autopsy photographs, the equation changed. If before John's letters to me, filled with generosity and childlike curiosity, had weighed on one side of my conscience, the photos fell like an anvil on the other, shaping my understanding of the crime like a putty of flesh and clotted blood into living nightmare.

When I heard what went on inside the apartment, I knew it was a different kind of crime from any a town typically experiences. But the crime itself wasn't unique. It's happened—infrequently—all over the world: parents killing their children. Less than two years before, Andrea Yates had drowned her five children in a bathtub in Houston. In 2009, a San Antonio woman killed her infant son and ate part of his brain. There are too many of these horror stories to enumerate. They happen, and then they happen again. I didn't pick the story of Julissa and John Stephan and Mary Jane because it was necessarily any worse than the rest, but being in my backyard, it exerted an unusual pull, one that didn't seem to let go, more than a decade later.

I eventually took a breath and returned the stack of photographs. One of the members of the office staff pulled down an unassuming cardboard box that contained the bloodstained knives that had been used in the murders and informed me that if I wanted to peruse its contents, I'd need a mask and some gloves. I declined.

Instead I went home and took another shower. I had nightmares that night, and every night for a week. Before I'd go to sleep, I'd start telling myself not to think of the photographs, and soon I could think of nothing else. They'd come at me in fragments and I'd try to blot them out, to invent another image that would collapse them into nothingness. But no image was powerful enough to supplant them.

Even after the nightmares subsided, I couldn't wear the shoes I'd worn when I walked around the apartment. They stayed in my home for weeks, sitting near the front door. I'd tie the laces, willing myself to leave with them on, then replace them at the last second. Then I gave up putting them on at all. I left home for a few months on a temporary assignment and took all of my clothes with me, except that dark gray pair of tennis shoes. I told my boyfriend I didn't need them anymore. When I returned to the apartment and unpacked my things, I noticed the shoes, waiting for me in the back of the closet, defiant.

"I thought I told you to throw these out," I said to Chris, though it felt more that the shoes had decided to stay of their own volition.

He looked back at me, confused. They weren't old, nothing was wrong with them.

I put them in the garbage.

The remnants of what had happened were long aged—nearly a decade had passed—but I couldn't wear the shoes that had tread on floors where so much blood was spilled.

When I walk around any big city, I know I'm stepping in the prettied-up path of bloodshed. It might be possible to trace a murder to every block in some neighborhoods. Reflecting on our nation's origins, founded on murderous theft and enslavement, every valley and plain recalls a spilling of blood, a bad history that surrounds us, silently begging to be recognized. Sometimes it seems easier not to know. Easier to forget the murders and the bloody concrete, the remnants of DNA, the graphic histories of violence, to live in a world where the horrors of the past are invisible, or else you'd have to throw out your shoes every time they touched the street.

Another letter arrived from John. I held it between my fingertips, looking at it the way Minerva regarded me when I'd told her I'd gone inside the apartment—as if something might rub off, something that couldn't be washed away.

Julissa

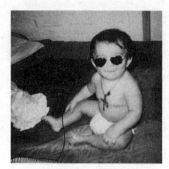

John Stephan

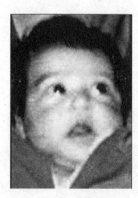

Mary Jane
*(Photos courtesy of
John Allen Rubio)*

CHAPTER 13

Belief

Can the devil make you do things?
I don't know—I thank God for that.
I've never been in that predicament, and I hope and pray
that I never will be in that predicament.
—LUIS ORTEGA, SWIM TEAM COACH

What was that intangible darkness, the tar that seeped through my skin, when I went inside the building? I didn't sense it the first time I visited, as an uninitiated reporter with no attachment to what had happened there. Minerva said I needed holy water to erase the damage from my trespass. I'd sought none, but had begun to doubt whether I could put what I'd seen behind me.

While I'd noticed the *hierberias*, little storefronts downtown that sold herbs and amulets used in folk healing, I'd never had a reason to spend much time inside one. As a reporter, I'd covered Ash Wednesday, when worshippers spilled out of the Immaculate Conception Cathedral with wavy crosses on their foreheads. I'd gotten dizzy with heat inside a sweat lodge and followed the teenage girl dressed as the Virgen de Guadalupe raised on a float and carried through the streets each year on December 12. In one of my first assignments for the paper, I went to a backyard in the Southmost neighborhood to write about an image of the Virgen that had appeared on a woman's tree trunk. My questions had been almost comically superficial: How does it make you feel to have the Virgen here in your backyard? Why do you love her so much? I approached these rituals as an outsider, unsure how to engage in a conversation about convictions to which I couldn't relate.

But as I got deeper into my inquiry, many of those I interviewed described the metaphysical connection to what had happened and its legacy. The attorneys had seriously considered a defense of devil possession. John and Angela had practiced the ritual of the *huevo*, the egg, the night before the murders, to determine if evil was in Julissa. The neighbors had diagnosed the building with a spiritual cancer, which they said continued to run through it, untreated. The role of spirituality was central and yet ethereal, a set of dots I couldn't connect.

One day I went into a *hierberia* on Market Square. I'd passed its hand-painted yellow sign many times before, with the Eye of Providence peeking out from the top, a deck of tarot cards spread along the bottom. Inside were the statues and candles used to create altars, and the herbs that might be prescribed by a folk healer for a cleansing tea or bath. Some of the items were familiar—chamomile or clove—which you could also find in a supermarket, while others were more obscure. Here were statues of Santa Muerte, the death saint, who had become stunningly popular in recent years in Mexico, partly because it was believed that she delivered results expediently and responded to requests purer figures such as the Virgen de Guadalupe would not. These statues are of a cloaked skeletal figure carrying a scythe and sometimes a globe to symbolize world domination. Many consider her to be a comforting, protective presence, so much so that they tattoo her on their skin. Inside the store, I spoke to a young man named Joe Uvalles, who said his grandmother was a *curandera* and card reader. A TV blasted the sighs and arguments of a *telenovela* as we spoke.

Joe grew up in Southmost and watched his grandmother minister to the people who came to her house. Only in middle school, when his friends began hanging out at one another's homes, did he realize, "This is not something everyone does."

Joe picked up his grandmother's techniques as he followed her to cleanse homes and treat clients. She had a gift, he said, an ability to intuit what ailed those who sought her counsel. As he grew older, he realized that he had the same ability.

Curanderismo, he explained, is not about curses or vengeance. "It acknowledges that there are negative things, that bad things exist, bad things happen to you. But at the same time its focus is sort of, the work is to cure, to heal."

Part of his job at the *hierberia*, when a client came in, was to determine whether the person was suffering from a genuine curse or whether that supposed curse was a scapegoat for the person's misfortune. One man, he said, complained that a curse had caused him to lose his job, but after intuiting he was free from any malediction, Joe concluded that the man's unemployment might more easily be explained by simple incompetence.

"They kind of become upset because you're not telling them what they want to hear."

Curandero Conversations, authored by Brownsville anthropologist Dr. Antonio Zavaleta, was recommended to me by Joe and others. Dr. Zavaleta had been studying folk healing of the border for four decades, and as a native of Brownsville, a scientist, and a spiritual man, he balanced the roles of insider and academic.

Dr. Zavaleta was partially deaf, and his booming voice moved with the rushed cadence of a busy, cluttered mind. Tall, paunchy, and verbose, he dominated whatever space he found himself in. I'd met him many times over my years at *The Brownsville Herald*—he was nearly always suggested by the university as an expert in subjects tied to local culture. But *curanderismo* was his true specialty, and one that he was often interviewed about when it came up in the news. Dr. Zavaleta was intensely open-minded, delighting in analytical discussion as much as anyone else I've met, but he could quickly put up a wall to protect the healers he'd spent his life studying. I didn't blame him: the knowledge they'd shared with him was sacred, and I wasn't committed to understanding these beliefs in the manner of a convert.

Curandero Conversations was his most open offering on the subject. In the book, Dr. Zavaleta shares a written dialogue with *curandero* Alberto Salinas Jr., who had since passed away. In 190 entries, individuals write in with their concerns, and Salinas responds. Dr. Zavaleta then adds commentary and context.

Most of the entries are related to concrete life events. People are reaching out for advice on the dramatic and the mundane, and symbolism is everywhere. A politician is running for office and worries when his opponent hires a *bruja* to ensure victory, but is relieved when a white dove appears in a dream. A person is losing his or her mother to cancer and wants advice on how to deal with such a loss. A parent is concerned about her one-year-old, who has suddenly gotten irritable, and speculates that the *mal de ojo* has been cast upon the child. Interpreting a strong look or an unusual dream is common in *curanderismo*, and seeing either as a cause of illness or bad luck is not considered paranoid; it's common knowledge that they are often connected.

In some of the entries, the clients openly discuss medical diagnoses of mental illness with the *curandero*. Early in the book, an unidentified follower writes:

> I was diagnosed with paranoid schizophrenia when I was a teenager and for years I was not able to attend school or function normally, to hold a job or to have a lasting relationship.
>
> My mother turned to spirituality in order to help me and eventually we were referred to you for help. Even though I take my prescription medications and see a therapist regularly, it was not until I began coming to you for counseling that I was able to keep my mental illness in check. My illness will never leave me but I know that you are protecting me from the evil spirits which surround me.

The *curandero* responds by thanking the individual for his or her testimonial, adding that the client's stability "should continue as long as you take your medication, see your therapist and place your faith in God." The *curandero* instructs that a candle should always be burning on the client's home altar and reassures that they have successfully built a protective spiritual wall. It's an ideal manifestation of the way folk healing and mental-health care can work symbiotically to achieve a stable outcome. It also upends a stereotype about the relationship between religion and mental illness: instead of amplifying this person's paranoia, the spiritual connection actually helps tame it.

But, in many letters, it's impossible to discern the true cause of the client's distress. Dr. Zavaleta volunteered that *curanderos* are in no way equipped to diagnose or cure mental illness.

"The *curanderas* are regular people, often your neighbor living down the block," Dr. Zavaleta said. "They don't have any special training. For the most part they have no training at all. They have a gift, and through that they're able to practice."

In the courtroom it became necessary to address the issue of possession and the authenticity of John and Angela's beliefs, to show whether they were invented so as to pretend insanity, or if they had an authentic connection to John's mental state. The prosecuting attorneys also seemed aware that some jurors might believe that a possession was responsible for the couple's actions. In his opening statement during John's first trial, Assistant DA E. Paxton Warner went as far as to tell the jury that the evidence presented would show that "there was no witchcraft that day, that his children were not possessed by the grandmother or any other spirit." John's grandmother had an altar in her home and he believed her to practice witchcraft, something he spoke about to Gina and his family. His grandmother's voice, he said, came out of Julissa's mouth that day in their apartment.

Dr. Zavaleta was called to testify during the first trial. He hadn't been given much information about the case beforehand, other than John's confession and a tour through the apartment. Depending on which parts you read, the testimony favors either the defense or the prosecution. When answering questions from the prosecuting attorney, Dr. Zavaleta indicated that, indeed, perfectly sane people can and do have religious beliefs, and that merely hearing God speak to you or seeing a family member in a dream does not indicate you are abnormal. He also said that John and Angela's apartment lacked an altar or complex collection of objects that would indicate a serious practice of witchcraft.

But when defense attorney Alfredo Padilla questioned him, Dr. Zavaleta allowed that possession is ultimately in the eye of the beholder, and that people who are not devoutly religious would be more likely to label such behavior as symptomatic of mental illness:

Q. And there is no guidelines and there is no manual to say, this is a possession, this is not a possession. It all has to do with how the person perceives the occurring act?

A. I think that's exactly correct.

Q. And whether this is a possession or not, there are certain individuals who believe that somebody may be possessed. And, again, there is no established criteria as to what possession entails; isn't that correct?

A. That is exactly correct. In fact, if you believe in possession, then you treat it appropriately. If you don't believe in possession, then you take the person to a mental health practitioner.

Q. And how that person reacts to the belief that a possession exists, a lot of times, is, again, we go back to that person and how that person perceived the concurrent act or the acts that he was able to observe, that's what we are looking at, what that person perceived. Because, I mean, what I may perceive can certainly be demonic, but may not be what you consider to be demonic. Isn't that correct?

A. That's correct.

Q. If the light burns out here and I may concede, well, you know what? That's a demonic act. Somebody in here produced a spirit, you know, to burn that lightbulb out. Now you may not have the same perception—you may not have the same belief, but I can feel real comfortable. I can sit here and say, "You know what? That light burned out because somebody out here in the audience, you know, put a spell on that light." And you're not right, and I'm not right. We just have different perceptions about the act, is that correct?

A, That's absolutely correct.

This is a crucial exchange. Padilla explains why it's so tricky to consider the role of religion in this case: a person's behavior, and indeed every act and occurrence in the world, can be the result of spiritual forces, or none whatsoever. It all depends on your perspective. It's impossible to make a judgment as to which perceptions are real, and which are false, without assuming your personal view to be more valid than your neighbor's.

Most people do not suffer from a "classic" case of mental illnesses like schizophrenia or bipolar disorder, but rather have an individual presentation of an illness or mixture of illnesses. Dr. David Novosad, a psychiatrist who often gives forensic testimony, told me that it's difficult to find a criminal with a so-called textbook case of schizophrenia, but that only such cases would likely cause a jury to find a defendant not guilty by reason of insanity. In a textbook case, a person who has grown up in a stable home has a sudden, clear, and otherwise unexplainable break from his or her former behavior, experiencing the delusions and hearing the voices that are hallmark symptoms. But many schizophrenics, such as John, also use drugs or have had traumatic experiences in childhood, making it challenging to pinpoint the start and cause of specific behaviors.

"We don't really understand a lot about mental illness," said Dr. Novosad. He works in a state hospital in Oregon with three categories of patients: the involuntarily committed, those charged with a crime but too mentally ill to work with an attorney, and those found not guilty by reason of insanity. Dr. Novosad said that, even for psychiatrists, clear-cut diagnoses are elusive, a reality that's not palatable in the legal arena. That's why reading expert testimony from John's trial is so confusing. Different psychiatrists deliver divergent evaluations of John—that his behavior was the result of schizophrenia or spray use or some combination. That he was not schizophrenic at all, that his behavior in interviews showed he understood his life and was not governed by delusions. The truth is potentially impossible to pin down because drugs can trigger mental illness and can also make people behave as though they were mentally ill. While the high from spray use is short, and John said he'd not huffed in several days, some psychiatrists would argue that brain damage from such chronic use can alter behavior after the initial high is gone, mimicking an illness such as schizophrenia.

Dr. Raphael Morris described a laundry list of John's symptoms during the second trial. It muddied the water for the jury, while also getting closer to a realistic description of his mental state.

"I picked up on different symptom clusters related to delusions, related to hallucinations, related to mood, related to sleep disturbances, related to concentration, distractibility, restlessness. His substance-abuse history was also very complicated. He had used different substances, mostly spray paint and marijuana, but I know there had also been positive urine tests for cocaine at some point. So I was trying to get a thorough substance-abuse history, and also taking that into consideration in forming an opinion about his mental state and what were the driving forces in his behavior; basically, doing a—trying to do what I call—what we would call a thorough risk assessment."

So many details are presented at a trial like John's, it's difficult for a jury to weed through such testimony and determine how much to blame John's choices or his illness for his actions that day.

"They want certainty. As an expert witness, you will lose if you express uncertainty," Dr. Novosad said.

A forensic psychiatrist who often testifies in New Jersey courts, Dr. Daniel Greenfield, told me that successful testimony has as much if not more to do with effective communication as it does content: "I've seen highly qualified experts go down in flames because the jury didn't understand what they were talking about." The law, he said, is often incompatible with scientific nuance. To further complicate matters, attorneys naturally seek out experts who they expect will support their theory of the case. In the Northeast, where Dr. Greenfield works, "lawyers rely tremendously on word of mouth. Certain people develop reputations for being mainly prosecution witnesses or defense witnesses."

Dr. Morris was among the experts to conclude John had paranoid schizophrenia. The delusions both he and Dr. Valverde elicited, he testified, "have to do with making these unrealistic connections, seeing something that—a sign, a picture, a person on the bus, and then folding it into his system and misinterpreting it, thinking that it means something that it doesn't mean, like that there is a danger, that there is witchcraft, that there is possession."

This is some of the most persuasive psychiatric testimony I read in John's case. It includes all of the behaviors that often coexist for those with serious mental illness, painting a picture of a troubled person with many layers of symptoms. Ironically, these can cancel one another out for a Texas jury trying to decide if the legal definition of insanity has been met.

Among US states, the legal components of the not guilty by reason of insanity defense vary. Some states don't allow the defense at all. Many, like Texas, use the M'Naghten standard as a template for their definition. It originated in 1843 during an English court casc in which Daniel M'Naghten shot and killed a man whom he believed to be the prime minister. Though English law had long had room to protect those who were mentally ill from punishment, the incident forced the courts to create a clearer definition. The resulting M'Naghten standard required the defendant to not have known the nature of the act he or she was committing. If he or she did know the nature of the act, then he or she must not have known it was wrong. In his book *Insanity: Murder, Madness, and the Law*, Professor Charles P. Ewing writes, "The M'Naghten standard, like the insanity defense more generally, has proven controversial but enduring. More than 165 years later, this test (or some variation of it) is still the law in the majority of American jurisdictions."

Texas's derivation of the M'Naghten standard states, "At the time of the conduct charged, the actor, as a result of a mental disease or defect, did not know that his conduct was wrong." In New Hampshire, the Durham Rule is used, under which the defendant can be found not guilty if his behavior was the "product" of a mental disease or mental defect, a vague definition that all other US courts have rejected. Still other states use the Model Penal Code, developed by the American Law Institute, which requires that the defendant must be diagnosed with a mental disease or defect and was unable to either appreciate the criminality of his or her conduct or conform that conduct to the requirements of the law. This defense lost much of its support in 1982, however, after John Hinckley Jr., who attempted to assassinate President Ronald Reagan the previous year, was found not guilty by reason of insanity.

In my own home growing up, the most prominent belief system in our day-to-day life was the reality of mental illness and well-being, a framework that has powerfully shaped how I've seen the world. Both of my parents are therapists, and they felt a personal, moral obligation to their work that I found inspiring. While our society still tends to see physical health as a concrete reality and mental illness as a questionable, almost mythical concept, in my upbringing there was never any question of its importance or potential deadliness if left alone or inadequately treated. That is the lens through which I see this case: I am more likely to put primacy on John's mental health than a spiritual force that might have taken hold. That doesn't mean I discount the role of spirituality. Both religion and mental illness are deeply personal, and a chasm will always exist between what one person experiences and another perceives.

In John's case, an amalgamation of religious references, drugs, and mental illness conspire to make it nearly impossible to definitively answer which of the following four scenarios is correct: John was lying about his belief that the children were possessed; the possession was real; John's use of spray caused him to have symptoms similar to schizophrenia; or finally, John's mental illness caused him to believe the children were possessed. Perhaps there are more scenarios than even these four. As Padilla said to Dr. Zavaleta, "You're not right, and I'm not right."

John himself laid out this ambiguity for detectives in his confession shortly after the crimes.

> Q. Okay. So what is the—what is the reason you are telling us that you killed your children?
>
> A. Because I want to tell the truth.
>
> Q. But what is the reason that you're telling us that you killed them? Why—what is the reason that you killed them? What is the reason that you killed them?
>
> A. Because, one, they were possessed. Two, maybe I kind of think it might have been the toxins that were there, the fumes that got me dizzy, but I don't know. I think it might have been more than one thing, sir.

The truth can be more than one thing. The potential targets of blame seem to combine and then explode, and in the wake of that catastrophe it's impossible to put the pieces back together again, to parse them out and name any one as the culprit. We can't know whether, if one part had been absent—the drugs, the mental illness,

John's early abuse—the others wouldn't have combined and delivered the same result. This not-knowing is agonizing; it means a man may be put to death who was insane at the time of his offense. And how reassuring it would be to discern what singularly prompted his actions and then to be able to devote oneself to stamping it out.

Dr. Zavaleta, who refused to shrink down the complexities of folk healing to fit inside the courtroom, was not asked to testify in the second trial.

The most important message he wished to convey, in this case as in any other religiously related murder case he'd been asked to speak about as an expert, is that a bold line separates *brujería*, or witchcraft, and *curanderismo*, or folk healing. *Curanderismo*, that healing side of the coin, is not solely a religious practice, but derives from the medicinal healing that was performed before institutional medicine and has continued to be practiced alongside it. In the United States, people might be more familiar with the term medicine man, a healer whose treatments are intertwined with spirituality, and who uses herbs with powerful properties.

Dr. Zavaleta and I met at La Azteca, a *hierberia* owned by Ruben Garcia, a longtime student of world religions. The two men explained that the religious and healing practices of South Texas are a mixture not only of indigenous beliefs and Catholicism, but also Judaism and Afro-Caribbean religions, a *mestizaje*, or mixing, of global culture. It's the story of the Americas, broadly. As I listened to them catch up and debate definitions, I felt as if I were sitting in on a graduate seminar. Both men had abundant experience and knowledge, and Garcia kept saying the phrase "so much," struggling to convey all of the background and complexity I couldn't possibly glean during my short introduction to these practices.

At the end of our conversation, they talked about the most famous *curanderos* from across the region, naming names they wished to be left off the record. Many had passed away.

Garcia seemed suddenly tired at the thought of these dead healers. He worried that the art of *curanderismo* would soon evaporate into pharmaceutical remedies and false impersonations. None of his sons were interested in the knowledge he had to pass along, and he expected it would die with him.

"They have other professions," he said. "One of them works in medicine, okay, and he believes, okay, that everything have to do with pharmaceutical things and all that. They believe that. So plants is totally different. But, I mean, the secrets of the plants are so incredible."

The way John and Angela interpreted the *mal de ojo* and use of the *huevo* did not fall into Garcia's definition of authentic *curanderismo*. While John and Angela used the egg to diagnose evil in Julissa, Dr. Zavaleta said the use of an egg by a *curandera* would remove the ailment, and no one except a *curandera* would be able to divine a message by cracking the egg open.

It was almost offensive to Garcia and Dr. Zavaleta that the case be lumped in with *curanderismo*, as had so many others in the past, unfairly attaching a stigma to traditions full of healing and hope. John and Angela knew only enough about *curanderismo*, Dr. Zavaleta said, to be dangerous.

Like many people with paranoid delusions, John, as Dr. Morris indicated, seemed to cherry-pick aspects of the world around him and amplify them into a self-fulfilling and fungible logic, in which he was selected for an important purpose—the "chosen one," as he told many relatives and friends. Religious symbols, altars, and concepts such as possession made it into the mix of John's delusions, but so did horror movies and his hamsters. Religion is a natural fit for the delusions of schizophrenics because it relies on unseen forces that can't scientifically be proven. The level of religious delusions experienced by those with schizophrenia varies widely by country and culture, according to Dr. Philippe Huguelet and Dr. Sylvia Mohr of the Geneva University Hospitals. According to their article, descriptively titled "The Relationship between Schizophrenia and Religion and Its Implications for Care," in *Swiss Medical Weekly*, 36 percent of schizophrenic inpatients in the United States had religious delusions, versus 7 percent in Japan. While at times such associations can worsen patients' symptoms or prompt acts of violence or the rejection of psychiatric care, religion can also help many to cope and stave off suicide. *Curanderismo*, which aims to heal, can of course mutate in the mind of an ill person. But it could help them as well.

"*Curanderismo*—it's so pure, it's so white, so light. There's so much light in it," Garcia said. When he looked at what happened on East Tyler Street, he saw only darkness.

CHAPTER 14

CHAPTER 14

The End of History Illusion

History, it seems, is always ending today.
—AUTHORS OF "THE END OF HISTORY ILLUSION" IN THE JOURNAL *SCIENCE*

John initially refused an in-person interview with me, but I felt sure that meeting him would offer something his letters did not. I worried that writing about his life without meeting him would be a disservice: without that face-to-face, he was an abstraction, a collection of words and pictures rather than a whole human being.

I asked John if he might reconsider letting me come visit, and he wrote back, saying yes.

I have refused to have interviews because of the reasons you know of and for some dumb reason most people take my regret and shame when talking about my kids as if I am lyeing but really it is that I can not look at a person in the face without wanting to brake down. It took a great amount of will to not lose it in the trial, since I was already emotionally drained because I cryed myself to sleep almost every night it was easier to compose myself.

As I prepared for our meeting, I watched video of his being interviewed in 2010 by forensic psychiatrist Dr. Michael Welner in preparation for the second trial. In the tape, John sat in the corner of a blank beige room. His ankles and wrists were shackled. He wore an orange jumpsuit and rectangular, thick-framed glasses. His dark hair was thinning and slicked back, and his face was rounder and fuller than it had been seven years before, when he was arrested. He looked, from the neck up, normal.

Thick black pouches that looked to be made of a synthetic material like nylon were over John's hands, a security measure so he couldn't use his fingers. The psychiatrist explained the procedure to John slowly and deliberately. John sat patiently. When asked if he understood, John told Dr. Welner that, yes, that he'd been through all of this before many times, and that he'd been tested since he was young when he was in special-education classes.

Before the examination began, John asked if he could take his own notes.

"I think that again," Dr. Welner began, "if there are certain secure policies about us sitting together here, and I have no objection to you writing notes, but I'm concerned about abandoning those—"

"It's been done before," John interjected.

"I know that it's been done before, but I've never met you, so if it's been done before with us, it must have been my past life. We're meeting for the first time. We have a videotape in order to make a record of our encounter." Dr. Welner sounded as if he were talking to a small child. In some ways his tone made sense—he didn't quite know John's level of intelligence. But judging from the way John pursed his lips, he was used to being belittled this way. He looked as if he was watching an act he'd seen before and didn't enjoy the first time.

"It's tiring and it kinda hurts to repeat the same things over and over again," John told the examiner. "I don't try to think about certain things, you know, it's pretty hard. I know that this needs to be done so I'm going to do it."

The video had a disturbing symmetry. Dr. Welner was offscreen, his voice the only evidence of his existence. Like him, I asked John questions about his life, but I was always out of the frame. I had control. I listened to John, but he didn't ask questions. He seemed to know the rules.

The examiner's voice was gentle, but when he started asking John questions, they seemed to hit him like stones—with a sharp and blunt force. Name this month. Now start naming the months of the year backward, starting from this month. Now memorize these three phrases. Repeat them to me. Tell them to me again in a few minutes. What's today's date? What medications are you taking? Where are we? Why are we here? What does it mean when someone says, "The grass is always greener on the other side"? John struggled with some of the math, but answered almost everything correctly. He seemed used to answering such questions.

Dr. Welner moved beyond those kinds of questions, used to establish intelligence and ensure that John understood the content of the conversation, and began to talk with John about his early life. Dr. Welner asked him about dancing in high school. "I used to love dancing," John said. "It's just something that would make me feel better; because of all the exercise and everything I felt my mind clearer. It's like a washing away." He talked about his life before jail—

the dances and swimming, the ROTC meetings and girlfriends—as if they were preserved in amber.

I'd recently read about a study that showed people have a hard time predicting what they will enjoy in the future. In the journal *Science*, psychology researchers from Harvard, the University of Virginia, and the National Fund for Scientific Research in Belgium, named this phenomenon "the end of history illusion." Their study found that most people believe they have come to their true preferences at last and won't change again. It's a form of present-tense narcissism, a vision of one's current self as the best and most advanced model possible. The researchers hypothesized that the illusion derives, in part, from the failure by most people to give time and its influence sufficient credit.

Time is a powerful force that transforms people's preferences, reshapes their values, and alters their personalities, and we suspect that people generally underestimate the magnitude of those changes. In other words, people may believe that who they are today is pretty much who they will be tomorrow, despite the fact that it isn't who they were yesterday. In the studies we describe here, we showed that people expect to change little in the future, despite knowing that they have changed a lot in the past, and that this tendency bedevils their decision-making.

John was looking back at his life. But from an outsider's perspective, the murders created an "end of history illusion." What could he tell the interviewer of the past seven years of his life since the murders? If his preferences had changed from age twenty-two to twenty-eight, what would that meaningfully translate to, and would anyone care?

The study points to our inability to recognize change, even in ourselves. If people can and do change, parting from our past selves inevitably and imperceptibly, was it possible to see the John of today as someone distinct from the crime he had committed? Was it ever possible to see a person as separate from the things he or she had done, or was his crime an indispensable part of him, one that couldn't be obscured or parted from, even for a moment? Maybe this man, the one with a knife, sweating, bloodied, with wild eyes, would stand next to him like a double for the rest of his life, leering at him and anyone who might want to talk with him again. Maybe that's what fairness looks like—one's mistakes are present, incapable of true erasure. The stain they leave is a warning.

The question underscoring all these others presented itself: Did John deserve to die for his crimes? That is, the two Johns—the one who committed this act, and his present self, the one who would lie on the gurney, containing the other within. I started to feel that this decision, of whether he deserved death as punishment, was one I had to make, even if it would have no influence on the outcome. I didn't sit on the jury that sentenced John to death, but he is not going to be killed by a juror or a judge. He is going to be killed by a representational democracy, the citizens of which support the state's ability to wield a power usually left to forces beyond our control—the ability to decide who shall live and who shall die.

I, and you reading this, we are compelled to decide if we want to kill John.

I need to look him in the face.

CHAPTER 15

Place of No Return

Our time here is so short.

—OFFICER EFRAIN CERVANTES

I flew to Houston from the East Coast, where I was visiting family. I rented a car when I landed and drove through the soupy August heat. It ought to have taken me thirty minutes to make it from the airport to my hotel, though with bad directions and worse traffic the drive took two hours.

Fresh cookies and lemonade were cheerfully arranged on a table in the lobby. I'm going to death row, I thought, as I took a bite of a cookie. A bartender poured a tall, cold beer in the hotel bar, which I carried up to my room. There, a king-size bed was made up, expansive and white like a clean canvas. Scented soap and lotion sat next to the bathroom sink, and a flat-screen TV was on the wall.

I'm going to death row tomorrow.

I slipped into bed, intending to fall asleep early. Instead I stayed up watching a movie I can't recall.

In the morning, I drove an hour north to the prison, a blocky series of featureless structures, ringed with shimmering layers of barbed wire, set off from a country road.

I'd come with the basic provisions that blogs and friends recommended: a Ziploc bag containing two rolls of quarters, driver's license, and keys. I'd dressed conservatively and brought an extra sweatshirt for the air-conditioned room.

An officer popped the hood and trunk of the car and checked for contraband. At a small security building, another officer stripped the paper wrapping from the rolls of quarters while I walked through the metal detector. I was given a long chain with a yellow tile marked 11, and I put it around my neck. I walked through the back door, away from the first barbed-wire fence and toward the prison. Back outside, the sky was cloudy, the sun pushing through the gaps of gray. The path between the buildings was lined with flowers, zinnias, a woman later told me. Bright and healthy, and growing happily in the sunlight. I wanted to take a picture of them, but I had only my eyes. I looked at things carefully and tried to remember.

Inside the prison, a drawing of the singer Selena adorned the wall, along with portraits of horses with the names Wimpy and Leo. Two thick metal security doors closed heavily, leading to a room that recalled a high school cafeteria. Tables and a line of booths were in the middle of the room, where the inmates were carted in and placed in individual cells. Large windows framed the trees and sky outside, though the inmates couldn't see these from their vantage point. The effect was of a peninsula of prison cells the size of phone booths, jutting out into an otherwise unremarkable cafeteria.

I received the number of a booth where John would be brought, sat down at the chair in front of it, and waited.

Next to me, a middle-aged white man with glasses and a trim beard, dressed in khakis and loafers, sat in front of the Plexiglas, explaining the work of comedian Larry David to a prisoner. First he talked about a *Seinfeld* episode—that one where George is worried he's slighted a waitress. Then he explained the plot of *Curb Your Enthusiasm*. His description approximated to "Larry David always says exactly what you'd be thinking in that situation, but would never say out loud." I marveled that this constituted death-row conversation. It also released me from the nervous certainty that talking to John would be bleak and awkward. This man was explaining one of the most frivolous shows on television to an inmate, and the story didn't seem to have much of a purpose other than as shared conversation.

Then, the prisoner brought a furry arm up to the glass, along with a note written on a piece of paper the size of a cocktail napkin. Among the scribbled phrases I made out "Where Does the Money Go?" The man in the glasses murmured in response. He seemed uncomfortable.

To my right, a middle-aged woman, African-American, petite, with long hair and high heels, vigorously affirmed what the inmate to whom she was speaking said. Yes, he had been placed in jail based on shoddy detective work. Yes, his associates were the real perpetrators. Yes, there would be justice. Or at least that's the impression she presented from the visitor's side of the glass. She spoke in legal jargon—perjured testimony and affidavits. Based on the small sliver I saw of the man—a wildly gesturing arm—he seemed young and strong.

Down the row, a young couple with similar short blond hair-cuts and ambiguous European accents had come to visit an inmate. They were joyous, laughing with a man who appeared to be a treasured friend.

The vending machine was an important aspect of the visiting ritual: it offered a chance to pretend at normalcy—sharing a meal and conversation with a brother, a father, a friend, the way you might in the outside world. The options—sandwiches, slices of pie—were more like items you'd find at a picnic than typical vending-machine fare, and visitors asked prisoners their preferences, paying and then having the items delivered by a guard to the booths.

I'd been waiting for forty minutes when a blur of white clothing moved into my line of vision. John was escorted into the booth by a guard. John's smile was interrupted only for a moment as he put his hands behind him through the slot of the booth so the guard could remove John's handcuffs. When his hands were free, the smile returned.

John's smile was warm, beaming, and unnerving. I didn't want him to be so happy to see me; I worried at what it meant. But I smiled back reflexively. I tried to find a middle ground, between a smile and a serious look.

What is it like in here? I asked, or some approximation of this question. John said he was allotted ten hours of outdoor time a week, split up into five two-hour blocks. He had slots in his cell, so he could speak with other inmates. He got rotated every six months to a new area of the prison, so if he made a friend or an enemy, he wouldn't be next to him permanently. The prison was often noisy, and he said he heard screaming. Despite the time ticking away, the noise and constant light in his cell didn't give him much chance at sleep.

John's face was round, his hair thin, shorter than it had been during his last court appearance, and he wasn't wearing the thick-framed glasses that he wears in the courtroom. He was pale and looked unhealthy, like someone who'd spent too long on a sea voyage and lacked basic vitamins. At thirty-three, he'd lost the sharp features of his youth—the strung-out, wiry twenty-two-year-old with a shock of thick dark hair was long gone. He was padded with extra weight, complained of regular sinus infections, and carried eye drops with him. There was nothing remotely threatening in his manner. He was just a person, carrying around complications and contradictions, warmth, a desire to relate to another human being. He may have also been "manipulative" and "self-serving," phrases I remembered from professional assessments. But we both had our purpose in the room, and if he was helping himself, he was helping me, too.

John's voice reminded me of others I'd heard in the Rio Grande Valley, a distinctive cadence to the rhythm of his speech; the best description I can muster is English spoken with the musicality and pacing of Mexican Spanish—a Texican accent. In his booth, he sat in one position for a time and then shifted, creating awkward contortions with his body to get comfortable and simultaneously hold the phone, on its short cord. What had changed since he went to jail, ten years ago?

iPads, iPhones, cell phones, he said.

Yes, I said. *Everyone has the Internet on their phone, and they're on it all the time.*

We'd started on an easy topic. But his smile was bothering me so I moved on to the serious questions. We talked about the kids, the idea that they were possessed. He said he used to have a recurring dream that he was being attacked by demons. In it, he would cut off their heads. When this happened with his children, he said he believed they, too, were demons and acted on impulse. The dream seemed as if it had become reality. There was more to these discussions, but as I wasn't allowed to bring a recorder or anything to write with into the visiting room, much of our conversation is lost.

I asked John what he wanted from the vending machine. He didn't know. He'd been short on visitors.

I've always liked cheesecake, he said.

There was no cheesecake. I remembered the death-row blog; the inmates rarely had meat or fruit in their diet. I returned with fruit, a sandwich, dessert, and a soda.

I asked him more about details from his letters. He remembered a dance he'd done with a group of other teenagers at a party, where they dressed up as the aliens and secret agents from *Men in Black.* I laughed, imagining this. I should have expected it, based on his writing, but I was amazed how friendly John was. Even in this dark and depressing place for an interview, the visit was a relief from the tedium of his cell. He finally had the chance to both physically and mentally escape for a few hours without a psychological examination, courtroom, or attorney involved.

John told me that his mother still believed he was innocent of the crime. His uncle Juan had told me that he thought there could be some other explanation for what happened, and John was taking the blame for someone else.

I'd wondered if John's learning disability would prevent us from having a complex conversation, but he spoke fluidly. It made John happy to think about his children, he said. I believed him. His face lit up whenever he spoke about them, and his expressions grew more animated, as he lovingly imitated the way Julissa talked, for example. These relationships were the most unblemished in his life. His children had loved him. They would never know what had become of him. John Stephan and Mary Jane were probably too young to understand what was happening when they died that night. Unlike with John's brothers and mother, whom he'd caused grave anguish, and with Angela, his relationship with his children was preserved.

At times my questions confused John, or he seemed hesitant to answer. He'd look at me sheepishly or sometimes smirk. Alternately, he would brag, making a point to talk about his talent at fixing computers or drawing cartoons, though usually with a self-deprecating dimension to the story. While he asked me few questions during the visit, the ones he did pose made me realize just how little he knew about me, even after years of correspondence.

Is this the first time you've been on an airplane? he asked.

No, I fly a lot because my family is on the East Coast. I didn't tell him about my recent vacation, or virtually anything about myself. Some of his psychiatric evaluations had indicated he had narcissistic tendencies, and I wondered if his lack of questioning was related to mental illness, or if he was just attuned to my reluctance to talk about myself.

Due to the long journey, I'd requested a four-hour visit, double the normal allotment. While four hours seemed like an eternity when I entered the prison, they moved quickly. Soon the guard walked up and told me it was time to leave. Neither John nor I had realized we were so close to the end of the visit, and as I said good-bye, John seemed to be in shock—the time was gone, and he wasn't prepared for it to end.

I walked out of the prison, each door and gate opening slowly until I finally reached the parking lot. The delicious feeling of freedom, like the purest rainwater, washed over me as I drove away. My life was in my hands. It was a great responsibility—to care for it, value it, and protect it. Not to waste it.

In those hours John came across as a childlike, charismatic, friendly man with a desire to convey his story. This image matched up with the persona in his letters. Of course, I didn't really know him, and the story he told of his life was contradictory and one-sided. Still, as much as I might question his motives or his truthfulness or the way mental illness might impact his behavior, the visit had achieved its purpose: he was no longer a collection of words on a page, he was a three-dimensional, talking, thinking, feeling person, and meeting him made something click. To see another human being and hear his life told to you in his words, with a desire to be known and understood, is to acknowledge that life, and so, too, the weight of his death. Personally sending John to that death became inconceivable.

As I left the prison, I took out my tape recorder and tried to remember everything—every impression, every phrase, every question. But in time those recollections faded, and even the recording I'd made became flimsy and disposable compared to the reality of sitting inside the prison, listening to John speak.

• • •

Capital punishment has morphed many times in the history of the United States. An earlier American incarnation—lynching—was often perpetrated by communities and individuals outside the realm of the law and was tacitly supported by the government, which failed to prosecute it. Though capital punishment was legal in some states even then, the mob lynching—without the time and due process of a trial—was more popular during its height.

Today, the death penalty is carefully administered and, compared to other political issues so inextricably tied to morality, causes a surprising minimum of drama. Many people have never deeply considered their position. The United States has no single standard. In some states the death penalty was abolished long ago. Others apply it in their own aberrant fashion; in Pennsylvania, almost two hundred inmates are on death row, but since 1990, when the method for death was switched to lethal injection, only three people have been executed, and no one has been executed since 1999. Most death-row inmates across the United States go through an extended, arduous appeals process, exhausting all avenues that might prevent their execution, and most of those sentenced are never put to death, with the exception of those in a few states, such as Texas.

Dr. David Garland, a professor of sociology and law at New York University, examined this paradox in his book *Peculiar Institution: America's Death Penalty in an Age of Abolition*. Today, the nations that apply capital punishment are outliers, and so, too, are the US states that regularly carry out executions. Most of the developed world has abandoned the practice, considering it outdated and an assault on human dignity. America's death penalty is peculiar for many reasons, but crucially because it derives from a well of emotion—fear, revenge, sadness—that it does not directly answer to in its contemporary application, when execution is delayed for a decade or more after the crime and conviction because of appeals. A crowd, crying for blood, no longer watches the event, as it once did at the guillotine in France or at hangings in England, or at some of the lynchings in the American South. Instead, the inmate is led into a hospital-like room and secured to a gurney before the lethal injection is administered. The inmates are treated, as Dr. Garland notes, much like patients in a hospice—with respect for their privacy and a minimum of pain. Of course, this is all its own brand of theater: an intentional death of a healthy person made to look more like the mercy killing of a sick dog or cat. The pretense of magnanimity at executions prevents the martyrdom or sympathy that might be generated by a more torturous slaughter.

Dr. Austin Sarat, a professor of political science at Amherst College, authored *Gruesome Spectacles: Botched Executions and America's Death Penalty*, which chronicles capital punishment gone wrong through the centuries as the United States has attempted to find a more "humane" form, moving from hanging to electrocution, poison gas, and lethal injection. Even when using this final method, the state, Dr. Sarat found, can only pretend at an ability to control death: an alarmingly high number of lethal injections are especially painful or prolonged—from 1980 to 2010, Dr. Sarat put that figure at more than 7 percent.

Who is being put to death at such executions? It is and is not the person who committed the crime. Decades may have passed.

The person in the gurney may have become devoutly religious, or new evidence may have complicated the way the person's crime is understood. The sentenced may have gotten married to someone who doubts their guilt or forgives them. Or they may be even more bitter and ruthless, and less repentant. Of course, as is disturbingly often the case, they may be innocent. Since 1973, one person has been exonerated for every nine executed, according to Dr. Sarat.

Change may also have occurred on a larger scale in the community where the crime took place, with the criminal act receding into the distance. In the popular justice of the past, this community, as a mob, fueled by outrage, ended the life of an alleged killer. The mob often employed extraordinarily graphic violence to do so. These acts—burning people to death, slowly cutting them into pieces, pouring boiling oil into their wounds, and other methods used independently and in combination—were remarkably imaginative and intended to surpass the brutality of the original crime committed. The waiting period inherent to the modern application of the death penalty makes it possible for the emotions that drove such acts to subside. A new generation comes of age. The punishment of the convicted becomes secondary to current issues of concern, including whatever new transgression has been committed.

Some of those who support the death penalty say they do not want to pay for the criminals to live in prison. According to Garland, the costs of keeping someone alive in prison are far exceeded by those incurred when the death penalty is pursued, in large part because of the cost of the original trial, which is much lengthier and includes more expert testimony and far more attorney hours. Subsequent rounds of appeals continue to escalate the cost. A study by the Urban Institute using data from 1978 to 1999 found that Maryland spent about $1.1 million for each death-penalty-eligible case in which prosecutors did not pursue this sentence, compared to about $3 million in cases that resulted in a sentence of death.

Perhaps, in a state such as Pennsylvania, the existence of the death penalty, though unapplied, maintains a purpose: sentencing a criminal to execution is a symbolic means of affirming to victims and citizens that the person accused is deserving of the maximum punishment available. Death is delayed, dangled over the convicted, until they die of natural causes in prison.

Texas is not Pennsylvania. Here, the death penalty is not an empty threat; it is a frequently applied punishment. The gap between how these two states use it indicates what has allowed the penalty to survive in the United States: the division of state and federal powers. A majority of Americans may or may not approve of the practice. That doesn't matter—the majority of Texas lawmakers do.

Michael Graczyk, an Associated Press reporter based in Houston, has witnessed around four hundred executions since 1984, perhaps more than any other American and certainly more than any other journalist in this country. He describes executions, using the lethal injection method, as somewhat anticlimactic. The person usually begins to make noises that sound like snoring. Eventually, the sounds get less pronounced, and the person stops moving.

In Texas, the members of the family of the victim and the family of the convicted are placed in two separate rooms, where they watch the execution from behind a window. By the time they are allowed into these rooms, the needle has already been inserted into the arm of the convicted. No appeals are possible, just the inmate's last words. After the execution is complete, Graczyk often asks the family of the victim how they feel, and they sometimes express disillusionment: the execution took too many years to complete, they lament, and when it was actually carried out, it appeared to be disconcertingly peaceful, like the "dude was taking a nap," as one man said to Graczyk.

Witnesses chosen by the convicted often shed tears. Sometimes they beat on the walls or cry out or hyperventilate. In many instances, by the time the execution is over, a foggy handprint is on the window.

The victim's family, on the other side of the wall, tends to show less emotion. Graczyk can remember few occasions when these witnesses have done more than simply sit in silence. At one execution, a man turned his back toward the convicted, so it was all the condemned man could see of him as he died. Once, when the execution was completed, an observer yelled out, "It's time to paaaaarty!" Usually, however, little is said. The day that began this process— when the loved one was killed—hangs over the event and likely dominates thoughts. It might be seen as a victory—that justice has been served—but it's also solemn, a day of mourning for a series of events that all wish had never transpired.

The intentionally mundane nature of these executions usually gives reporters little material to sensationalize, were they so inclined. This suits Graczyk well, as a careful steward of this controversial beat, intent on maintaining impartiality. When asked how the executions weigh on him, the emotions he goes through, or the experience of watching the first execution versus the four hundredth, he said that his work as a reporter preempts any possibility of emotional involvement. He is simply too busy doing his job, often as the only reporter present to record what transpires, to indulge personal revelations.

I asked Graczyk if it would be useful for me to attend an execution as I attempted to understand them better.

"The only thing that you would see or experience for yourself is how quickly it occurs," he said. Normally, the inmate goes unconscious in less than a minute. Ten or twenty minutes later, a physician comes in the room and pronounces him or her dead, but the precise moment of death is unknown.

I asked him again—would there be something to understand, not as a reporter gathering facts, but as a person experiencing the event?

Graczyk said he didn't understand why I would want to attend an execution unless I had some personal stake in the case, as the witnesses typically do. He was right: Who would want to watch such a morbid event? Who would want to impinge on the privacy of the families as they mourn? A reporter attends on behalf of the public, to monitor this most powerful symbol of the state's control—its ability to take life. But don't I and every other American have a personal stake in every execution that occurs? How can any of us discover our position on such a law without comprehending its full weight, as we might if we saw it enacted?

The viewing of executions was once essential to their power. In France, the usefulness of the guillotine depended on the crowd and its reaction. During the Revolution, these public executions became such a popular part of life that a crowd of regulars convened daily to watch, the operators were celebrated, songs were written about the instrument, and a child-size replica with a real blade was a popular children's toy. Public executions ended in France in 1939—three years after the final public execution in the United States—though capital punishment remained legal there until 1981. While in retrospect the guillotine is a stark symbol of state brutality, it was considered the most humane method at the time—a rapid drop of a blade meant to end life as efficiently as possible. Now lethal injection is considered more civilized, but the guillotine was likely a quicker form of death. As Dr. Sarat writes, "The experience of execution by its witnesses—their 'suffering'— fuels the search for painless death," more so than the desire to curtail the torture of the convicted.

Graczyk has mostly numbed to the horrors that prompted the executions he reports on. After his reading and writing in detail about hundreds of murders, only parenthood has changed his perspective, giving him a heightened awareness of the vulnerability of his children. When they don't show up on time, he imagines the worst, knowing that the scenarios his mind might invent are more than hypothetical. The worst has happened and will likely happen again to some child.

"You try to tell your kids, without scaring them, that there are bad people out there," he said.

In Brownsville, the building on East Tyler Street is a reminder of such atrocities. Though inanimate, its voice resonates. Carlos Garcia, the chief of police in Brownsville when the children were killed, told me that, while the Rubio deaths "should teach us a lesson, some will learn and some will never learn." Garcia kept his composure through nearly an hour of discussion about the crime scene, his own children, and the violence he's seen in his career. Only when we came back to the role of the building did he break down. "It should remind us that life is precious, that our children are precious to us, and to go home and hug our children every day," he said tearfully. "If the building stays behind, it will always be a landmark of three children who were never given an opportunity to live, to see the sun rise one more time, to see the moon."

Larry Lof, who has restored many of Brownsville's most famous buildings, told me that the architecture in a community adds up to more than the sum of its parts. "A historic neighborhood is a collection of buildings. None of them might be the most special building in town, but together they form an *ambiente*, they form a character that defines a neighborhood."

What would be lost if that voice, an insistent whisper, was silenced? Under Lof's definition, any building the city demolishes represents a small blow to Brownsville's history. I imagined an aging woman's face, then a brow lift, collagen in the lips, stretching of the skin. Now she is unrecognizable.

Though I sometimes thought of John when I looked at the building, and the time both had left, their respective ends were in no way equivalent. To kill a person exists on another plane from the act of dismantling bricks and wood beams. The parallel is found in the satisfaction promised by destruction: to lend the weight of tangibility to the ephemeral. You can take a mallet and bust into the wall of a building. You can load poison into a syringe and inject it into the body of a human being.

You can see them both reduced to absence. Then, we are left with nonexistence, a blank space. A piece of earth can host another structure, and though it will be different from what came before, it can serve a new purpose. But when a life is gone, it is not replaced.

I returned to see John a year later. He was still going through post-conviction review, but he likely had less than a decade left in Livingston before he would be taken to nearby Huntsville to be executed.

As I drove toward the prison, the small hills began to get more pronounced, and trees blazed red and yellow on the edges of the road. I didn't feel nervous this time, as I had the last. Still, certain facts were churning in my mind: I wanted to know more about John's spray use, which had been far more excessive than I'd realized, and ask him about the state of the apartment—perpetually filthy in the months before the children died, and shared with other people who were doing drugs and working as prostitutes.

My visit fell on the Tuesday before Thanksgiving, and several of the visitors at death row were children, ranging from a towheaded toddler with a sparkly headband, to a teenager play-fighting with a younger sibling. The mood was somber, and again the conversations for the most part had little to do with the prison that surrounded us. People seemed intent on pretending that they were not using a telephone to communicate through the thick wall of glass that separated them from their loved ones who sat, depersonalized, in plain white jumpsuits. No, we were just sitting in a cafeteria, munching on pastries from a vending machine, catching up before the holiday. I heard a father talk about car mechanics, and a teenage girl describe getting noticed by boys in the neighborhood.

Stay cool, I love you, a man said over the phone, putting it on the cradle as he smiled through some private pain.

An hour later, John was brought out and placed in the little booth in front of me. Once the barred door was closed behind him, a guard removed his handcuffs through a hole in the back of the miniature cell. John smiled, and I smiled back. He told me that I looked tired.

"It's a long trip," I said.

He looked tired, too, though I didn't tell him so. Dark bags were under his eyes, and his skin was pale, his hair shaved close to his skull. His cheeks had a couple of days' worth of stubble, which he said he'd been punished for. He'd gotten in trouble in the past for setting fires in his cell.

John was happy for the break from his quarters, but he seemed fundamentally sad. He asked me how things were, and I told him that I got married a couple of months before, and that I was planning to move away from the valley. He congratulated me. I asked him how he'd been and he said okay. One couldn't expect a better response than that. No one in here was doing "well" or "great."

I've never huffed paint and asked John what it felt like. He said that huffing was ultimately not about pleasure. It was a distraction, albeit one that lasted only minutes, from an emptiness he'd felt inside in his teens and the first years of his twenties. After graduation, the boundaries of high school, the coaches and the teachers who motivated him to come to practice, study harder, get in shape, were absent. He had no direction at home, and high school was the closest he ever came to thriving. His attention problems and learning disability got in his way, and he was unhappy when bored. Of course, the spray and the pot likely made this worse.

John remembered how his attention problems had made it difficult for him to concentrate on the tedious, repetitive jobs required at fast-food restaurants. He wanted to be challenged, but he seemed to lack the ability to create manageable challenges for himself. The army, he felt, was the solution. But the test required for entrance necessitated three hours of intense concentration, and this obstacle, he said, was impossible for him to overcome.

When John graduated from high school, life was unstructured, and perhaps like a typical eighteen-year-old, he thought this freedom was exactly what he wanted. He could spend his days having sex, doing drugs, with few responsibilities. Though never medicated for a mental illness before prison, John was deeply depressed, and when Gina broke up with him, the malaise deepened. Drugs were a coping mechanism, and he relied on them more and more. His brief stint with prostitution, he said, was something he tried to get out of his funk, in addition to earning money.

John looked back at his teenage self, regarding his behavior as both juvenile and entirely explainable. He could see why the army seemed like a good fit, why he needed boundaries more than most kids his age. But when he was young, he didn't understand why he was turning to drugs, why he needed but rejected structure. He remembered his special-education teacher, Ms. Treviño, the one he had called Mom. John wrote to me:

She cared and scalded me for slaking off, saying I could do better.
It was because she believed in me that I tried harder than I felt like

doing. I wanted her to be proud of me as my own mother did not praise me for the good I would do, often anyway.

He had been eager to settle down—having two common-law wives in quick succession—but was also restless. With both Gina and Angela, John took on not only a relationship, but an instant family as well. With Angela, that meant both a one-year-old daughter and an infant on the way. These children were the brightest spot in John's life; maybe they represented a way to fill the void, to create a sense of purpose.

Shortly after John's arrest, and his diagnosis of paranoid schizophrenia, he was put on several medications. He told me he was taking Prozac, for depression, Benadryl, and Risperdal, an antipsychotic. This made it hard for me to know what an unmedicated John sounded like. He said he had occasional visions, what some might call hallucinations, but these days he tried to ignore them, a self-preservation technique schizophrenics sometimes use to deal with an illness that can be manageable but is never curable. He said that the two years following the crimes, the visions were much worse, and his sincere wish was to die and join his children in heaven.

I did not get the sense that John was trying to manipulate me, but I'm not a psychiatrist. I can't be sure of the authenticity of John's presentation. I can only go on what experts told me, and what I've read.

I bought him some food during this second visit; a guard delivered it again. On John's forearm was a tattoo, ANGIE in wavy letters. John said he'd got it inked a couple years after his incarceration.

Now, long after Angela had stopped communicating with him, she still remained in his sight line every time he looked toward his hands.

Psychiatrists who evaluated John for the trials found him to be narcissistic, and to have delusions about his life. At times John made statements that seemed self-aggrandizing, mentioning, for example, that he was the good one in his family, and that since he'd left, depriving them of their moral center, they had fallen apart. He didn't seem to appreciate the irony that perhaps his action rather than his absence might have destroyed them.

Dr. Valverde said John had a "naivety" and that he was a "child-like soul." Though John occasionally got confused, Dr. Valverde said he never felt that John was lying to him, but merely searching for someone who would agree that what he did was "the only course of action he could have possibly taken given the circumstances." Dr. Welner testified that John had "a very interesting vulnerable charm that doesn't hit you until you've been with him for a little more than an hour, and then you really recognize yourself, as an interviewer, that you feel really taken by him."

Even while looking out for and recognizing that "charm," which suggests within it an ability to manipulate, I found it difficult to feel any vengeance or vitriol toward John, even long after I again drove away from the prison. It was easy to be angered, even sickened, by twenty-two-year-old John, and how his reckless choices had culminated in destruction all around him, but his life now was limited and marked at every corner by these failures. He hadn't outrun them; rather he dwelled inside them and would never escape. Maybe these fantasies of grandeur were a symptom of his illness. Maybe they

LAURA TILLMAN

were an escape mechanism that sometimes succeeded in granting temporary relief. On this visit, John seemed to be in mourning for all that was irretrievably lost.

The main message he tried to convey to me, one that he'd talked about during our first visit, was that he was never the calculating killer he'd been portrayed to be by the prosecution at his trials. He was guilty, and he didn't evade his guilt. He didn't necessarily think of himself as mentally ill, though it is common for paranoid schizophrenics to lack insight into their own illness. He wasn't ultimately sure if he'd killed the children because they were actually possessed, or what else might have catalyzed the event. But, he insisted, none of what transpired was premeditated, and it filled him only with sorrow and regret.

John didn't testify about the murders themselves during either of his trials, which is common in criminal cases. If he had, he might have asserted this position—that he did not believe himself to be insane—or a medicated John may simply have seemed too coherent to square with a jury's idea of what a crazy person sounds like. It was frustrating for him to sit in the courtroom listening to an evaluation of his life and his actions with no ability to weigh in.

During our conversations, John never "acted crazy." The little tells he gave, such as the way he sometimes smiled inappropriately when we approached a difficult topic, or his somewhat flat affect, didn't surprise me. Dr. Valverde said at trial that John's constricted affect was normal for people suffering from schizophrenia, who might have difficulty demonstrating to the world what they feel on the inside.

• • •

The jury did not have the option of sentencing John to life without parole at either trial, a choice now available in all states that have the death penalty. This change has added momentum to a quiet consensus that the abundance of deficiencies with the implementation of capital punishment—racial discrimination, wrongful conviction, botched execution, and high cost—outweigh the personal belief that putting a person to death in retribution for a crime is just.

"The result is that the death penalty is withering," Dr. Sarat told me. "It's dying on the vine."

Though the use of the death penalty has significantly decreased, the likelihood of abolition remains distant. It would require us to reckon with a different set of questions.

At the second trial, attorney Ed Stapleton finished his closing argument to the jury by introducing the concept of the "magic mirror."

"I meet someone and I hate them. And the tendency will be that I will hate them because of defects that I myself have. I think that guy thinks he's smarter than he is. See how it works? I meet someone and I love them. And what I see in them is qualities that maybe I have a little bit of." Stapleton implored the jury to look inside themselves and then look at John, "a man who has steeped himself in fear or been steeped in fear since infancy. His primary emotion, I would submit to you, from the evidence, is fear. And to allow that to be my primary emotion in dealing with him would not do justice. I would submit to myself. I need to look to the better parts of myself if I'm going to look at him and make a decision about whether or not there is any sufficient mitigation to save the man's life."

Stapleton spoke to a jury that stood in for the rest of us.

The death penalty has grown more deceptive over time. A person falls asleep. His neck is not snapped, he is not stoned or sliced apart by a falling blade. But the endgame is the same: he or she is dead, and as a society we must accept responsibility for the death, as the application of death as punishment is hardly a foregone conclusion. Of course, most of the time, the person on the gurney is also responsible. They've set this series of events in motion long ago. But acts do not exist in isolation in our world, and we can't expect to repair the misconduct of the past tidily, believing our response to also be contained. We are connected—invisibly, intricately, marvelously, and tragically—and those connections cannot be willed away. It would be satisfyingly simple to see an act as abominable as murder cured or avenged by putting the perpetrator of that crime to death. But the killings continue. They amp up— into school shootings, terrorist acts, wars that rage for decades. The question is whether one death addresses another, or whether they circle into a frenzy.

Perhaps the death penalty can be rationalized with a concise argument: some criminals deserve death. It doesn't matter if the death penalty doesn't actually deter murders or if it wastes millions of dollars. Taxpayers are willing to foot the bill because the person being put to death has done something so terrible that we as a society are obligated to end his or her life. Here, we are left with the question of death itself, one that must be decided individually: What is the import of avenging crimes with death? It's not a decision that can be made for any of us, but rather one that must be determined by each of us in the chambers of our conscience—quiet or chaotic as they might be—because it's a judgment that hammers on the center of so many moral dilemmas we face. To decide, we must consider how we view our station on earth. Do moral absolutes exist, or is the world grayer than we would generally like to acknowledge?

Is the question of whether death deserves death simple, or is it troubling, scratching at the doubt that lives in the pulpy center of our bodies, that mutable place that's capable of morphing?

Isai Ramirez
(Photo by Laura Tillman)

Minerva Perez
(Photo by Brad Doherty)

Alejandro Mendoza
(Photo by Brad Doherty)

CHAPTER 16

In the Garden

*I used to believe some people desirve daeth because of their
heart being so cold and evil but who of us is beyound repentance,
can not God do anything and change anyone?*

—JOHN ALLEN RUBIO

I took a drive to Brownsville on a muggy day, the sky a haze of deep
gray that made the little houses downtown look like unfinished figures in a charcoal drawing. I'd been traveling for two months, and
they had been good ones, filled with family and friends. Yet, when
I drove up behind the building and saw the stairs had been ripped
off and replaced with plywood, the backyard stripped of grass and
converted into raised garden beds, I felt as if I'd missed something
important, and the place had changed when I turned my back. I'd
tricked myself into believing that I'd mastered it with my mental
energy, memorizing its form.

The building had had a good summer, too. Families were planting
vegetables and herbs in the garden beds and flowers to attract butter-
flies. A row of benches had been built under the shade of an awning,
and the space was tidy and inviting. The garden had accomplished
something unexpected—it made the building seem beside the point.

The story of what had happened here lent strength to this new incarnation, a symbol of renewal in a spot where death once reigned. A large sign, facing the street, announced that this would be called the TRES ÁNGELES COMMUNITY GARDEN. Three angels—in honor of the children. The story had been modified by a single word: angels. Angels do not haunt. They protect. Angels bless. The change was startlingly positive, moving the dead from hell to heaven.

The power of the living over the dead was cruel in its totality. The dead could make no claims on how they would be remembered. They could only wait silently as the living adjudicated the nature of their legacy. But then the cycle would continue, until those now alive joined the dead, each new generation living at the cusp of history until forced to surrender their power to an unstemmable tide of new life.

As for the lives of Julissa, Mary Jane, and John Stephan, they had not been erased. The new garden indicated that still more history was to be written on this piece of earth. Life-sustaining vegetables and herbs could grow here. The living would not stop for the dead, but they could acknowledge the existence of both in the same space.

I called the number on the sign and spoke to the man in charge of the garden project, Dr. Wayne Wells. I wanted to meet him at the building.

"The tragic building," Wells said, his voice set back in his throat.

In October, Wells and Rosie Bustinza, the garden manager, walked me around, pointing out the crops that the members of the garden were growing in raised beds. Climbing spinach, healthy and prolific, shared space with broccoli, cauliflower, and cilantro. Peppers, eggplant, and basil, tomatoes and okra, crowded together in the boxes.

Wells said they were still hoping the building would come down, and that a little park with a memorial to the children would take its place. "We're hoping for January," he said. "They promised us they won't disturb the garden."

The city held a christening for the garden. Refreshments were lined up on a table, and the audience sat underneath a tent facing the garden and the building at its side.

"We're celebrating restoration, we're celebrating future harvests, and we're celebrating being together," Dr. Belinda Reininger, a professor of public health, told those gathered. "I know every time I have a visitor here I'm showing it off. I think it's a place that's not only transformed this local community, but Brownsville in general."

A couple of the gardeners got up and spoke about their experiences. Then Chris Patterson, the burly Parks and Recreation Department director, took the microphone. "For the longest time you drove by here, wondering what was going to be here," he said earnestly, "but you also got this empty feeling, just an empty feeling. A really dark feeling—I did. We started doing the community garden, and slowly but surely, it was like life was coming back. And so now I actually drive through here every morning just to see it."

Patterson tentatively read something he had written for the occasion. Stumbling a little, he began, "The cycle of life. All life begins, living things all have a moment at which time they become alive. That beginning of life marks the first point on the circle of life. This garden is the first point on the new cycle of life, this neighborhood. It is quickly bringing life back into this area. It was once a dark, dreary, empty lot, home to vagrants, rodents, and trash, and I should admit, a lot of that was here. It is now a lively, fresh, green sanctuary full of life. This event marks the start of a new life for our three little angels, who live in each root and stem and leaf of each plant in this lot. This neighborhood is now alive," Patterson said, as though, through these words, he was granting an unspoken wish. He urged everyone to keep the space clean.

Mayor Tony Martinez, a short, slim man in his sixties, with tailored clothes and a mop of shiny gray hair, walked to the podium. Martinez spoke warmly to the people of Brownsville, the proud parent to every girl and boy in the audience.

"This is gorgeous for the community, and when I say the community, I mean you and me. I don't want anybody to kind of walk out of here going, like, 'Well, that's a nice neighborhood but that's not my neighborhood.' Every neighbor is your neighbor, every brother is your brother, and every sister is your sister. We are the human family. There's nothing that divides us. There's nothing that makes us apart. We may be short, we may be tall, we may be a little chubby, we may be a little bit thin, whatever it is, but we're all the same. And so, that equality and that likeness of mind that brings that love out of your hearts, that's what I want to make sure that we allow to grow. If we want to do something from this point on, this is the first garden, but there's many more to come. But I encourage every one of you to spread the word. I want everyone to know about what you're doing here."

A previous mayor went on trial for allegations that he'd stolen money from the city and was acquitted. Martinez, with personal wealth and a clean reputation, seemed like a fresh start for Brownsville. He was paying more attention than his predecessors to beautification projects such as community gardens, hike and bike trails, and historic preservation. Brownsville had too many long-standing problems to be cured by a single public figure, but examples of progress were beginning to accumulate.

On Halloween, the city put on a party at the garden and the streets that surrounded it, in Barrio Buena Vida. Orange plastic pumpkins had been placed around the garden beds. Rosie Bustinza was there with her grandchildren, and they piled onto the benches for a group photo. She was buzzing with pride, both in her family and what they'd planted together. In the street, long tables were set up, and volunteers from the posh private school were handing out apples and bananas. As it got later, the streets filled with people. Toddlers wobbled in superhero costumes, and teenagers, covered in fake blood and wounds, watched their friends perform an exercise demonstration on a large stage that had been set up in the middle of the intersection. Again, the building was secondary. If the kids were aware of how jarring it was to see the fake gashes on their bodies in this setting, they didn't acknowledge it.

When I'd thrown away the shoes I wore inside the building, I recognized the irrational root of my action, but I couldn't resist the impulse. There was a nauseating immediacy in the contact between those shoes and the floor of the apartment. That Halloween, however, the faux-gory costumes signaled a change, a loosening of the grip the crime had on the neighborhood. It could be overlooked for an evening in the name of good-natured fun. Maybe one day the building would psychically blend back into the landscape, joining a family of other Brownsville buildings that had also survived, despite the complicated memories they inspired.

I walked around the corner, away from the celebration and

toward Minerva's house. She was there with her nephew Manuel, and they invited me inside. I asked her what she thought about the garden.

"It's nice, but they should tear out this thing," she said of the building.

The garden didn't change her mind?

"No." Minerva said that she'd been invited to plant a plot, but declined because she was often out of town.

"As long as you have that thing over there, there's always going to be a bad spirit," Manuel said. "They can have watermelons over there, they can have cucumbers. You need to understand one thing, the spirit—bad—is going to be over there."

Manuel said he walked by the building every day, sometimes late at night, and he could feel the spirits of the children as a physical presence. He could hear them, too.

"What do they sound like?"

"Like they're going to escape."

Minerva agreed with her nephew. "For us, we were here when that thing happened, we couldn't sleep for months! My mom was still alive, she was one hundred years old, she used to see the little kids go by to Good Neighbor for dinner or lunch."

Julissa would be sitting on John's shoulders, and Minerva's mom would hand out Popsicles to the kids.

Local politicians had made many promises to Minerva about the building. None had been fulfilled. It hadn't been destroyed, and while the garden had improved the back half, Minerva couldn't see that side from her house.

Mr. Mendoza, Minerva's lifelong neighbor, walked through the grassy lot that separated their houses and stood outside Minerva's living-room window.

"Acuérdate la güera?" she asked him, smiling. Do you remember the white woman? He did. I asked him what he thought about the garden. He didn't like it—of course. Mr. Mendoza never liked anything, by his own admission. His reaction made me smile—members of the garden had cheerfully told me about the time they'd spent cleaning up his yard.

"I'm not an outside man," he said. Also, he didn't like plants.

I walked with Minerva and her nephew down the street. The kids from the private school were still handing out fruit, while around the corner candy was distributed. Pop music blared and children in costumes and face paint swarmed around us, most demurring at fruit in favor of candy.

I told Minerva I'd gone to death row to meet John and that he'd told me he regretted his actions.

"I'm not here to judge him. The only one who can judge him is God," she said. "I know he did wrong, but we don't know what was going on in their world, you know. The only thing is, I feel sorry for those little kids! Because they were little angels, like all of these ones right here."

Minerva and Manuel and I wandered past the ballerina and bumblebee, the zombie and the Superman and the French maid. Minerva's memories of John were kind, and her desire to tear down the building didn't stem from vengeance or hatred, but from a subtler place. The deaths of the children were disturbing to her because she cared—because Julissa, Mary Jane, and John Stephan were real to her. So was John, a nice young man from the neighborhood. John was never disrespectful of her elderly mother, Minerva said, unlike some of the other people who stopped by.

"They're here right now," Minerva said of the children's spirits. The street was full of children who could have been the Rubio children, mothers who could have been Angela, and fathers who could have been John. She was right—they were all around us.

Proximity. That was key to understanding the crime's impact—and the limitations of that understanding. Minerva was physically close to the building, and more than that, she was sensitive and couldn't ignore its pull. I'd been trying to comprehend it, but when she asked me questions, challenging me—what would you think if you lived there? How would you feel if it were converted into an office and you had to work there every day?—I had to admit that I still didn't know what it felt like to be at the center. Maybe it would never be possible to transcend that final gap that separates us all from one another.

The picture was starting to meld. The building, the jail, the crime scene—yes. But also, the garden, the neighborhood, the commonality of childhood, the creases of history. It was astonishing to see the world as a single, quivering entity, rather than a set of various concerns parsed into distinct compartments. The murder and murderer could coexist with the rest—life, the city—and not be a feature set apart or used to demonize the inadequacies of the rest. It was one more thing, a sad and terrible thing, that happened to people, because of people, and belonged here along with the children picking leaves of climbing spinach from the vine, their grandmother Rosie standing by, full of pride. If it could be this way, integrated into the sprawling whole, then maybe it could be shaped like the earth, and there could be a modification of the human landscape. Maybe it could be a feature addressed as part of that whole. Tragedy is one more element, along with happiness, victory, grief, goodness, and on and on, in this pulsing, changing, densely connected human network that harmonizes and contradicts, all at once. Only then, when these events are not set aside on the shelf of the worst moments of the human race, and they become what they are— another element that is intricately bound—can we change. We can stop these crimes from happening, using the concrete tools and the subtler actions that often elude us. We can see children like Julissa, Mary Jane, and John Stephan grow up, and we can stop remembering victims as we choose—as angels or ghouls—and prevent them from becoming victims at all.

Already, this is happening in the little corner of Brownsville near East Tyler Street. There is a shift. You can feel it. That shift may be helping one family, or ten, to live a little better, have a little more support, so that they may evade a different kind of unfolding of their lives. It gives me hope that maybe this wasn't, as some people said, a sad story of evil, monstrous people. A story with no meaning. That's not the legacy of Julissa, Mary Jane, and John Stephan. Their long shadows make it possible to see the world more clearly, as neither pure light nor pure darkness, but a landscape where crest and valley are cast in shades of gray.

CHAPTER 17

Three Graves Together

*I told them that they got hurt by their parents,
and that now they are asleep and now with Jesus.*
—DIANA HERNANDEZ, CHOIR LEADER AT THE CHILDREN'S FUNERAL

In a grassy plain bordered by trees, John Stephan, Julissa, and Mary Jane lie quietly under nearly identical headstones alongside hundreds of other departed souls, just a few miles away from where they lived and died. Most of the graves in this cemetery have a container for flowers, and most of the headstones, embedded flat in the ground, are punctuated by the reds, pinks, and blues of artificial petals.

At the front office, I asked to be directed to the headstones of the children.

The secretary knew the spot. "The three graves together, just around the curve."

That visit took place early in the process of learning about the children, their parents who had come before them, and how residents across Brownsville had mourned and interpreted their passing. I'd never stood so close to them, but true knowledge remained far away.

In the seven years since I first stepped inside the building to the moment I arrived at the end of my inquiry, its fate had been in a constant state of uncertainty. The city had received a federal grant, which was used to purchase the building in 2009, with a plan to turn it into a community center. The endeavor was disorganized from the start. A struggle ensued to find an organization that would be willing to partner with local government to create such a center. The building's historic status complicated the issue—more red tape for any group that might want to take on its renovation. After several years, no collaborator could be found, and the city decided to return the federal funding in 2013, which would allow them to proceed with demolition. But just as it seemed the issue would be resolved, the new mayor, Tony Martinez, said he wanted the city to wait—with the creation of the Tres Ángeles Community Garden and its central location near the farmers' market came the hope that the building could one day be used for Brownsville's expanding health initiatives.

While this took place behind the scenes, the residents of Barrio Buena Vida witnessed the continued deterioration of a vacant structure where a tragic event once happened. A ten-year memorial service with the building as its backdrop further emphasized the lack of change. Many other possibilities were voiced—perhaps the building would be leveled and a park would honor the children. Maybe it could be used as a warehouse, an administrator proposed, to store parts of other restoration projects. Some hoped a colorful mural would brighten the exterior. Yet, years came and went and its doors remained shuttered. Even as the community garden brightened the back of the building, the interior collected new tenants—bats, Minerva had told me nervously—and rats.

The most promising proposal came from Melissa Delgado, who headed the Brownsville Wellness Coalition, and helped start the Tres Ángeles garden. Her positivity and determination were contagious: by 2015, more than 850 residents had participated in community gardens across Brownsville, a groundswell that sprang from that little plot on the corner of East Tyler and Eighth Street. The group planned to add several urban farms as well, and even a mobile unit that would bring fresh, local vegetables to residents in affordable housing. While Delgado initially felt that the memories attached to the building were "too sorrowful" for the city to proceed with any plan save demolition, she became increasingly convinced that the structure was the natural home for a community center for the Brownsville Wellness Coalition—a space that would host healthy cooking classes and serve as a base for the walking club, community garden program, and the farmers' market. The road to such a vision was long and fraught with potential complications. Shortly after her plan emerged, the city voted to proceed with demolition, after which the Historic Preservation and Design Review Board, which had replaced the heritage council, voted unanimously against demolition, a notable reversal from their original vote in 2008. Uncertainty continued, and the building sat, waiting.

I stopped by the garden whenever I could, visiting it along with the building. Usually the door was shut, but sometimes a gardener would let me in and casually give me a tour. One day, I met Isai Ramirez, a grandfather who had retired the month before from a career as a boat mechanic at the Port of Brownsville. A soft-spoken man with a gentle manner, he had a gray mustache and was dressed in jeans and a button-down shirt. He spoke proudly about his plot and held up a massive leaf of rainbow chard in wonderment. He'd never grown it before, but the plant was thriving. It doesn't taste very good, he said, but it's got lots of vitamins.

Isai was one of the first of the gardeners on East Tyler Street, and he'd felt a bad energy on this piece of land back then. "Every day you feel it less and less."

Isai looked at the building and down at his little plot of earth at its back.

"You just keep praying that you never get in that situation, you know, you or your family."

While I'd initially been skeptical about the community's motivation for destroying the building, wondering if it was a scapegoat for a set of troubling social issues Brownsville hadn't yet begun to resolve, things turned out to be much more complicated. The pain of seeing the building every day and watching what it was turning into, and therefore wanting it to be leveled, could be attributed to guilt. But in reality, the desire to destroy it wasn't an effort to pass off the blame. If anything, that impulse showed that the community was wounded by the murders, and they, too, wanted to heal. They wanted better conditions for the city's families, not run-down old structures.

The fate of the building was incidental compared to that of the lives that surrounded it, and the new projects aiming to provide sustenance and support for the families and children across Brownsville. There weren't enough projects, but there were more than there had been in 2003. The old challenges remained, but more people seemed to be working to overcome them, with a consensus that the problems of one were the problems of many.

A crime can unfairly define a community at large, the force of its violence blurring out whatever else might exist alongside it—the bystanders, the world afterward, the determination to prevent similar cases. In Brownsville, the response to what happened on East Tyler Street has been both moving and harrowing to explore. Maybe there is no purely right response when something so terribly wrong has happened. I struggle still to imagine how I might face a tragedy of this magnitude. I had the choice to learn about this story—it was not forced upon me.

The garden, with its name, Tres Ángeles, reflects an acknowledgment of the role the children have in shaping the city. They did not get to grow up, but they did leave their impression behind. Their presence here continues, with no end in sight.

It would be intolerable to spend all of our time examining the repercussions and roots of terrible acts. It would rob each of us of the time we have on this earth—finite, if we need reminding—to experience joy, to face our lives without fear, to be inspired and fascinated, and to feel deeply about our loved ones, rather than the life ended in another city far away.

At the same time, such crimes challenge us to think about who we are and whom we want to be to one another. At these moments, what would happen if we could dispose of the words that are so easy to fall back on when it's too exhausting to search for more precise language? What might become clearer when we draw into focus the blurry edges around the brutality? What questions might we voice for the first time? Such atrocities feel fresh to us and stun us into silence, but this process of questioning can keep us from reaching for that shelf where humanity's unimaginable violence is kept. It can keep us from closing the door. Tragedies such as this one threaten to obliterate subtlety, and in so doing, their suspected perpetrators become alien to us, often even when they are innocent. How can we expect to grant reasonable trials if we are so distracted by the crime that we label the presumed criminal "monster" and their actions "evil"? What insights do we miss when the initial shock of a crime causes us to look away and never revisit it again, except as one in a laundry list of regrettable events? A crime should never be used to define a community, but neither should it be treated as salacious and exceptional, requiring no further examination. We should demand a better world, and to do this we must better understand the world in which we live.

The events on East Tyler Street have become a part of people's lives, people who, like me, had no direct connection to John or Angela. I've spoken to many about this crime whose voices do not appear in these pages, people who were kind enough to share insights that helped guide my inquiry. I thank them, and all of those whose thoughts are documented here, for taking the time to talk about something so dark and difficult, with such generosity and care. Without them, I would understand nothing about the legacy of this case, one I initially viewed as a straightforward history of violence, and now know to reveal a city in which perseverance, optimism, and hope accompany even the darkest tragedy. Each conversation has led out in a dozen directions, linking up with a quote or image or feeling from days or months or years ago. This interconnectivity is striking—the way a crime both derives from and happens to us all, whether we are aware of it or not.

I've been unfailingly amazed by the power of time. I cannot

imagine trying to look at this crime in this way in its immediate aftermath. Time has given me the ability to interview people without the intense grief, shock, and rage that might have prevented us from speaking at all. It has allowed me to see the way people have changed, and the way the building has changed under their influence. Time may be a community's most valuable asset when trying to comprehend a terrible act that's shaped it.

The buffering effect of time is complicated. It can lead to forgetting, until the act is so far in the distance that memory of it disappears altogether, or the event transforms into myth. But time may also be the only salve that a family, of the victim or the perpetrator of a crime, has to heal a gaping wound. For them it's perhaps only by allowing that temporal distance to accumulate that the wound might turn into a scar.

The building drew me in, but the real pull was not the structure, it was the questions. I thought after all this time they would be resolved. Instead, I find myself more unmoored than when I started. Yet that doesn't bother me: resolution doesn't seem to be the purpose of questions like these. They open journeys, within and without, daring us after each step to go still further. The building on East Tyler Street is just a place where something happened. Its power lies in its ability to make present what is past, a past that too often contains events we wish were absent from reality. Ignoring these events does nothing to prevent them. And while the impulse to wipe the markers of their existence from the face of the earth is human, it shouldn't be misconstrued as a solution.

That day at the cemetery, the sky was clear and the air hot. A few small toys, which looked as if they'd been plucked from

Happy Meals, were scattered on Mary Jane's grave. The flowers were dirty, beginning to die an artificial death. But the place was lovely, in its way. A low mesquite tree provided a spot of shade, and I could see farmland in the distance. The grass and the lonely tree obliterated the violent images of the children that had been swimming in my mind. Here, at last, at least, they had a peaceful place to rest.

Acknowledgments

This book began with a seemingly misguided idea. I am indebted to the many people who offered encouragement and a healthy dose of skepticism. Both have been essential to its completion. Suzannah Lessard, thank you teaching me that passion about a particular topic is the most practical tool a writer can possess, and that a few thousand missteps are indispensable when on the path toward a project worth doing. Richard Todd, Diana Hume George, Tom French, Jacob Levenson, Leslie Rubinkowski, and the great Patsy Sims, thank you all for making the Goucher MFA program an unmatched home for literary nonfiction. Every residency I spent with you helped me to venture further, even when I didn't know where I was headed. To my Vassar College professors, thank you for providing the foundation that helped me tackle this subject.

My editors at Scribner, Nan Graham and Daniel Loedel, thank you for your fierce belief in this project. Every paragraph has benefitted from your insight and intelligence. Your rare sensitivity and willingness to embrace the ambiguous nature of this story have been a gift. In our work together, I've often felt as if I'm in a dream and might wake at any moment. Thanks to Jaya Miceli for the powerful cover, and Liza Longoria for her beautiful photograph, originally shot for

ACKNOWLEDGMENTS

The Brownsville Herald. At Scribner, a hearty thank-you to Elisa Rivlin, Colin Harrison, Brian Belfiglio, Kara Watson, Mia Crowley-Hald, Emily Remes, Steve Boldt, and Kate Lloyd for their dedication and enthusiasm at every turn, and to the many others behind the scenes.

To my agent, the incomparable Andrew Wylie, thank you for seeing what was possible and finding the right home for this book. I will forever be indebted to you for your unwavering confidence and wisdom. Thanks to the rest of the Wylie Agency, especially Jacqueline Ko and Julia Sanches.

To the staff of *The Brownsville Herald*, and to Rachel Benavidez for my first job in journalism, thank you for bringing me to the Rio Grande Valley. I count it as the best decision I ever made. Brad Doherty, thank you for all the images you've shot for this project over the years, some of which appear in these pages, and for your friendship. Thanks also to Macarena Hernández, Jennifer Muir, and Mireya Villarreal for talking with me about the experience of covering this case, and to Oscar Cásares and Cecilia Ballí for your insight into writing about the region.

I have so many people to thank in Brownsville, generally, but I have to begin with Yvette, Jojo, Blanca, and Joe Vela. You gave Chris and me a family in Brownsville, and we will always be grateful. Nadia Elfarnawani and Ruben Marin, thank you for your support through this process. To the many people in Brownsville whom I've interviewed, both directly for this book and over my years as a reporter, thank you for all that you've taught me. I imagine other places exist where there is such a concentration of kindness and generosity, but if there are, I haven't found them yet. To John Allen Rubio, thank you for sharing your story with me.

ACKNOWLEDGMENTS

Many people read parts of this book at various stages and gave me invaluable feedback. Justin Pope, Chris Sherman, David Tillman, Candice Lowe Swift, Theo Emery, and Abby Evans, thank you for so generously offering your time and insight. Kate Pumarejo, thank you tremendously for using your legal expertise to review mountains of court documents and ensure that I got the story right. Tom Colligan, my expert and persnickety fact-checker, thank you for your diligence and willingness to immerse yourself in such a difficult subject.

David Tavarez, Anthony Knopp, David Novosad, Daniel Greenfield, James Marcus, Austin Sarat, Antonio Zavaleta, and Mark Clark, thank you for our extended conversations on topics as diverse as historic preservation, forensic psychiatry, the death penalty, and religion, some brief glimpses of which appear in these pages. To Charles Eisendrath, Birgit Rieck, and Travis Holland in Ann Arbor, thank you for your inclusion and the great service you do for journalism. To Mark Schoifet and the late Fred Wiegold of *Bloomberg News*, thank you for taking the time to teach a lowly intern many valuable lessons about journalism and ethics. Thanks also to Dan Baum, for the early, essential advice that started me on this path in earnest. To the Sherman family, thank you for welcoming me in as one of your own. To my friends, with whom I've shared countless conversations about this project, you have helped me to think through problems big and small, and given me the extra push that I needed to continue—thank you.

I dedicate this to my family, especially my parents. Everything I am comes from your unwavering support and your example. I love you.

Finally, thank you, Chris, for your endless belief in this book and in me. I couldn't love you more, and then I do.